Henfryn

Henfryn

Radnorshire hill farming life in the 1930s and 40s

LOGASTON PRESS
Little Logaston, Woonton, Almeley
Herefordshire HR3 6QH

First published by Logaston Press 2002
Copyright © George F. Lewis 2002

ISBN 1 873827 08 3

Set in Times and Baskerville by Logaston Press
and printed in Great Britain by
Bell & Bain Ltd, Glasgow

Contents

Acknowledgments

I wish to acknowledge the constant support throughout of my wife, Vera, my daughter Shirley, my daughter and son-in-law Ann and Den, and my grand-daughters Donna and Karen.

For help in reminiscing, checking details and supplying some of the illustrations I would like to thank Mr. and Mrs. R. Barker, Dick Brick, Owen Ingram and family (Llawrllan, St. Harmon), Mr. and Mrs. P. Jones (Howey), Mr. and Mrs. F. Lawrence, Mrs. J. Lewis, Mrs. S. Lewis, Lucas Motorcycles (Ross-on-Wye), Mr. Bryan Maund, Mr. and Mrs. M. Morgan (Hafren furnishers), Mr. W. Morris, John Perks ('the gates'), Mr. David Powell (Henfryn), Mr. and Mrs. G. Powell, Mr. and Mrs. D. Price, Mr. and Mrs. K. Price, Mr. Noel Price, Mr. and Mrs. E.K. Pugh, Mrs. M. Williams along with the staff of Powys County Archives and County Library.

Preface

For years I entertained a half formed ambition to place on record some of the living conditions and social history in general of people in the rural areas of Mid Wales, something I considered to be lacking and which I was afraid would soon be lost with the passage of time. If I have achieved this I am well satisfied.

None of the people or incidents in this narrative is intended to be any other than as remembered, and in no way can this be likened to the Roman oration—'the evil that men do live after them, the good is oft interred with their bones'. Quite the opposite is intended.

CHAPTER I
The New Farm

The year 1930 saw an upheaval in my life. Early in the year I knew that something was in the wind, a sixth sense told me that a change was on the way. Eventually the news was broken to us children—my parents had bought another farm. What this was going to mean was not initially at all clear. My first thought was that I would have to go to a different school, with all the changes that that would bring. But coupled with this was the excitement of a larger and better farm with the associated pleasure of telling my schoolmates, though with a nagging feeling that there might be more to it than I knew at the time. Little did I think of the effect that it was going to have for me and my whole life.

Completion date was 25 March, a Quarter Day and a rent day—then a watershed in the life of most farms. Whilst the move officially took place on that date and all business was thereafter conducted from the new address, the family remained in the old place until May. During this period everyone lived at the old farm with the animals and machinery kept at the new, though we retained a couple of milking cows on a field termed the Boosey pasture to keep us with a supply of milk and butter. This was a common arrangement and it worked well, even though it entailed much travelling. It meant we had the buyer of our old farm by day and our own workmen at night.

The farmer of our new farm was retiring and so held a dispersal sale of his animals, machinery and equipment which gave us, the incomers, the chance to purchase that which we wanted. I was less aware of this than I was of the gathering of everything together on our old farm—tools, toys (not a big job) and pots and pans, crockery and furniture, everything that had been part of my life—whence it was taken by horse and cart to the new one. In their place the new farmer brought in his unfamiliar stuff.

In May the move was completed and each family in the chain moved to their 'new' farm and all rights as regards the previous were ended, unless of course there was a mortgage involved. The last load on the gambo included my old bike wheels with no tyres on and then the final blow—the 'sledge' or toboggan; it suddenly dawned on me that I would never, ever sledge down the 'Field above the House' again. I was also going to lose my hill, my place of freedom, my place of peace where I could see for many miles and breathe the air that was mine and mine alone. I'm not sure, but I think I went behind the house and had a little weep; even now writing about it it still has some emotional pull.

However, the biggest wrench of all, tempered with expectations, was to leave the school. The existing school was new, it had only been built a couple of years, but it was not so much the school I would miss as the teachers, for in some mysterious way they had become part of my family almost as much as my Mum and Dad. In addition, I would be leaving all my schoolfriends. I would have to face the unknown—a new world, uncertain and unpredictable and I knew that there was no going back.

The new farm was only three miles or so down the valley and the track to it skirted the hills and entered the holding on the eastern side. The way passed by what had been a couple of smallholdings, probably a pair of squatters' patches claimed under old squatters' rights. These allowed a newly wedded couple and their friends to claim all the land that they could enclose in a single night with a ditch, whilst at the same time building a house (which, due to the time constraints would consist largely of turves and drystone walling) which must have a fire in the hearth producing smoke from out of the top of the chimney by daybreak. The land that was able to be enclosed was very small, sufficient to keep one cow and her calf and so provide milk and a small quantity of butter. One of the two, the Camp, is now in a tumbled down condition and the other, the Vig, is just a pile of overgrown stone. Details of those who lived at the Camp are to be found in the county archives, but as far as I know no record of who lived at the Vig has come to light. Generally the occupier of such a cottage was a farmworker, with the produce gleaned from the 'smallholding' making life a little easier for himself and his family.

Top: The farmhouse at Henfryn towards the end of the 18th century
Below: As it was over 100 years later in 2001

My first sight of the new farm had been a bit of a let down. For a start the gate into the farm was off its hinges and had to be dragged open, whilst the land itself was covered with feg, a type of coarse grass that animals avoid, coupled with gorse, bracken and rushes. And all the hills in sight belonged to somebody else! There was not even the chance of my 'own' hill.

The farm backed on to an area of rough grazing called the Rhos—all I knew was that it was a pitifully poor exchange for our existing farm. The Rhos was covered with gorse, bracken, rushes, feg, abounded in banks and hollows—and contained two bogs for good measure. A few fields had holes in the hedges that two cows could walk through side by side. To say that I was disappointed would have been putting it mildly, but there was nothing that I could do about it and in any case I had full confidence in my Dad.

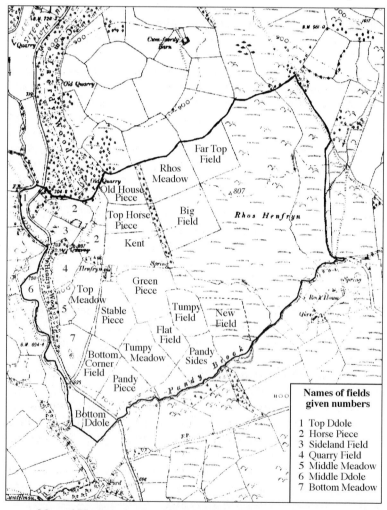

Map of Henfryn (within black outline) showing the field names

I had come to know that he never did anything without 'thinking it through', though at that stage his thinking and mine did not agree.

At least there was a decent sized field beyond the feg and f(y)ern, heather and gorse, in fact a field that was much bigger than I was used to. I could visualise plenty of room to play football without the ball ending in the hedge and getting punctured. At least that was a plus point; little did I then think of the length of the swathes of hay to turn with the hand rake or the length of the rows of swedes to hoe and thin. Another bright spot was that there were plenty of birds: curlews, peewits—plovers to the sophisticated, snipe, larks and pippits, and plenty of signs of rabbits, a source of possible income and sport.

Nearing the end of this rough ground on the day we moved in we came upon the cows, our cows and one in particular that made me feel a little more at home and that was Darkey, the old black cow. I am certain that she was also glad to see us. I feel that Darkey and I had some sort of affinity. My mother was unable to feed me as a baby, no doubt on account of the worry and stress at finding food and the rent, so Darkey was called in to deputise, via a bottle I hasten to add, making Darkey in effect my foster mother. Often when I was sent to bring the cows home for milking I would put one arm over her neck and hold back. She would stop and I would climb on her back and follow the other cows home along the way. If my Dad had found out he would have told me that I was too lazy to walk and to get on and do the job properly! (I was never told what happened to Darkey when she became old. I was too afraid to ask, and do not know to this day.)

Along with Darkey I could see Spot, so called as she had a brown spot the size of a tennis ball high and to the one side of her face. As this mark was a 'blemish' on a Hereford cow, she was bought cheaply, yet became the basis of a very good herd indeed, none of her progeny inheriting this mark. Then there was Old Sunnybank, bought from a farm of that name, 'Old' to distinguish her from her daughters Young Sunnybank and Little Sunnybank, the latter in fact no smaller than the rest. There, too, was the Grey Heifer, by then a cow many times over but she had kept her name. It was like meeting old friends and helped link the old with the new.

Beyond the cows was a gate that actually swung open on its hinges. I could now see the smoke from the farm's chimney, then there it was—the house. What a disappointment. I had built up an idea of a grand house because it was a bigger farm, but it was half hidden behind a hedge. I liked a house you could see, and what I could see was a silly house, one half of the long roof reaching down over the ground floor rooms and the other half ending at the upstairs level, and to cap that off, one big chimney and one tiny thing. They could have at least made them to look like a pair when they built them—we had had two nice big ones at Llan Nerch Freit (the old farm, now spelt Llannerchfraith) and for the life of me I couldn't see why there shouldn't be the same here.

The back door was where the long roof jutted out and made an angle. It would be possible to play football here like we did at the old place, but there would have to be a slight difference. Here the door itself would need to be the goal. One rule was soon in force: if you scored you had to clean off the resultant muddy mark to ensure further games. I remember one occasion when my brother was 'in goal'. I had taken a mighty drive when Dad opened the door, catching the ball straight in the chest like a top rank goalkeeper. It led to a temporary ban and a lecture as to what might have happened if it had been Mother who had opened the door at that moment.

Opening that back door on that first day, I did not care for the different smell which greeted me, prompting further doubts as to the future. But then I saw the pump just inside the door and the realisation flashed through my mind that there would be no more carrying water from the spout—what a dream. The pipes were rusted and the water proved only fit for washing hands, the well for drinking water being a hundred yards away, but half a loaf still proved better than no bread. But the ceiling! It was just bare timber, oh heavens what sort of a house was this? The floorboards of the bedrooms had just been painted over and right in the middle was a two inch square hole through which you could see the sloping ceiling of the bedroom under the eaves. I could see that some of the plaster had fallen off and the laths were bare where the plaster should have been. I was speechless. Later I was to find that the hole in the floor had a purpose—when the bacon pig was killed it was hung here by passing a chain up through the hole through which was then passed a spike, so holding the chain in place. It was believed that if the snout of the pig should come to rest on the floor on account of the stretching that took place, then the bacon would be spoiled and not 'Take' the salt properly.

But the worst was the colour of the place. The walls were green, a dark green all except where the smoke escaping from the baking oven had made it a sooty black. The copper or furnace was tucked away in the right-hand corner with a fire grate under it. A 6 inch glazed pipe in the wall let out the steam when the copper boiled, and was closed very effectively by a roof slate placed flat on it and weighted down by a large stone to prevent the ingress of rain, sleet or snow, and removed as required. At least once someone forgot to replace the stone, for I remember that a strong north wind had blown the slate off and, the snow swirling around, was then deposited in quite a drift on the lid of the copper.

A flue from under the copper took the smoke to join the main chimney. At least that was the intention, but if the wind was blowing in a certain direction it seemed that more smoke was coming down the chimney than was going up! No matter what the weather, when this happened the back door had to be kept open so that the washer woman or baking lady could have enough fresh air to carry out her duties. Fortunately a subsequent chimney sweeping session largely solved the problem—very much to everyone's relief.

When filled the copper would boil about 25 gallons of water at a time, a necessity when scalding the pig after it was killed to remove the bristles, or on Monday wash day.

The copper also had one other very important use. By this time harvest cider, at one time very cheap indeed, about doubled in price and was considered to be expensive to the extent that for us it put an end to the barrel of harvest cider for all time. To fill the gap it was decided to brew our own beer. My Father had helped when he was younger to brew 'small beer'—full blown beer was subject to excise duty, and who can imagine a farmer paying for the privilege of making their own beer? There again who could blame him if he tipped a dollop more of malt into the Mash Tub and an extra 8 ounces of hops in the boiling, just the sort of mistake that the poor old boy who didn't mean any harm could easily make, and a pound of brown sugar to every 5 gallons to make sure that the beer would 'Keep'— if it was allowed to!

The window over the sink already held all the appurtenances of a farmhouse window in this position: shaving gear, soap, soap powders and a mirror, this one cracked. The room also contained two scrubbed tables, one by the sink and the other along a wall and that had one leg out of sychronization with the others.

About turn and there was the dairy, the 'Cool Room' of the farm where the milk, butter, cheese and preserves, (jam and pickles to the farmer's wife) were stored, and to the left lay the kitchen. This room was the heart and stomach of the farm and all its operations— the nerve centre, control room, dining room, and rest room, and if there were children, the school room to boot.

A long oak table, bought at the dispersal sale and left where it had stood, was where we now ate our sandwiches and downed a cup of tea provided by Mrs. Price, the retiring farmer's wife. It was then that I noticed there were two grandfather clocks against one wall. Well, who wants two grandfather clocks, but if they do, then why in the same room and, more than that, on the same wall? Both were ticking loudly, for a while in unison, then gradually the one gained on the other until they ticked independently, and then one would be ticking whilst the other tocked until they closed in on each other once more. For a while I was amused by their ticking antics, but gradually this gave place to annoyance.

The oak table ran the length of the room, its thick polished top made from three planks. A bench one side would seat four people, and on the other was a window seat. After moving in a settle type seat made by my grandfather was placed in front of the window seat, completely hiding it, so as to provide more roomy seating for my three sisters. One hot summer's day, a few months after moving in and at hay making time, we returned from school to find absolute panic stations—all harvesting had been suspended as my youngest sister, then too young to attend school, was missing. We joined in a search of the house, the farm buildings, even the fowl houses. She was called for all over the farm, the river was searched, the road above and below the farm walked, but all to no avail. Eventually we all arrived back at base and went in to the house when my sister rises up from the hidden window seat, rubs the sleep out of her eyes and asks 'Is it tea time yet Mum?'. I leave the next five minutes for you to visualise in your own way.

Whilst we were eating our sandwiches Mr. Price was trying to tune his wireless and I had a good look at it, not that I was any wiser after than before. It had what was called a 'Cat's Whisker' which had to be fiddled with to find the point where the reception was best, and instead of a horn or loudspeaker it had earphones connected by two wires from the Cat's Whisker arrangement. How these wires could make sounds was beyond me, but I decided that by hook or by crook I'd find out some day. Mr. Price suddenly exclaimed 'Well, did you ever hear such a thing in your life?'

I thought this deliriously funny and burst out laughing, to be told afterwards that I had shown 'Very Bad Manners', the possession of their opposite was considered very important in those days.

Overall the kitchen had the same sort of 'set up' as that in the old home, apart from those two clocks, but was strange in the same way as a person you have not met before. It may look alright, neither liked or disliked, something or someone that exists without any connection or affinity, just like looking at a photograph of people or places of which you have no knowledge. This feeling lasted for some time even though mitigated by the presence of some familiar furniture and knick-knacks which, for a while, seemed like plants that had been transplanted and not yet grown into place. Gradually things grew to fit, like the healing of a wound that you were only vaguely conscious of and that healed without a scar.

Straight in front of us was the inglenook fireplace, very similar to the one at the old place except that the huge oak beam that supported the opening was much lower, causing many a lump on the head as we adjusted to it. As the window was quite small it reminded me of a dark cave with a great wide mouth.

In the opposite corner to which we entered the kitchen was a door to the front hall which was too small to swing a cat, assuming you could even see to try that out, for the only light was by the way of two small panes of glass set in the front door.

Across the hall was the door to the parlour, very small but cosy looking after the one we had before. It had a wooden floor with rugs on it, a nice little fire grate and shelves to put a few books on— I loved a fire and a book or two. This was the best thing I had seen so far.

Back in the hall there was another door, this one opposite the front door and, oddly to my mind, led to the stairs. I noticed that the stairs had one step less than the old set and, rather like adjusting to the low beam in the kitchen fireplace, I was forever taking one step more than was there or tried to step down another at the bottom.

Four bedrooms opened off a square landing, one big square one with a dinky fire grate, one very small one that was a true twin to the parlour, a third that was long and narrow and occupied the whole end of the house but only had one small window, and the fourth was some sort of an afterthought made after extending the roof and which only contained a small area where it was high enough for a tall person to stand upright. The head of the bed had to be placed against the wall where it was high and the foot reached nearly to the low wall under the eaves—and this was my and my brother's room. It also had the hole in the floor from which the pig was suspended, so either we had 'a modern ventilation system' that had to be covered with rugs, or the doubtful company of a huge heap of chain. The only window was at floor level, and where the ceiling was lowest.

The colour of the rest of the walls of the house shared one thing in common with those of the kitchen—they were dark, but brown, almost black, as opposed to green. When we moved in I grumbled away and whilst my brother, being older and stronger than me, had to work outside helping on the farm, I served my apprenticeship as a painter on those doors and windows. I even cashed in on it, for my grumbling led to a bribe to carry on, but it left another mark—to this day I positively hate painting doors and windows.

The original brown colour tended to be fairly universal on farms. Painters in those days made up their own paint approximating to the colour that was required. Waste was anathema, yet even to the old painters it was impossible to mix and make up the exact amount of paint to do the job and have none spare. So instead of leaving a drop in every tin (as we often do) to go hard and useless, a container was used to receive any spare paint irrespective of colour, bearing in mind that all the paint was of their own making and therefore compatible. The result was a brown paint of varying shades, though I fancy in our case that the painter had at some time mixed a lot more black than he required.

A few years later, as funds became available, the small windows were replaced with very much larger ones and in one case a new window was put in where there was none before and maybe you have guessed it—I had the job of painting that lot! All things come in threes, so said the old people, and so did these painting jobs. Two tins of a nice light green turned up, one of undercoat and one of gloss to do the outside of the house, and I was at it again.

In time a home grew out of and around the new place, but I am certain that I shall never know the new home in the same way as the old, and now after many years this is doubly true.

Some 30 yards through the gate by the end of the house lay the farm buildings with the track dropping gently towards them, and these at least looked better than the ones we had left behind. They were shaped like a letter L, but open at the angle which was where the track passed through. To the left of the passage, when coming from the house, lay a barn and storage for feed, grain and machinery, and on the right was stabling.

The barn was in fact only a portion of a complete range of buildings that included a hay loft, chaffing loft and granary on the upper level. The lower level included the Wain House where the carts and machinery was stored, and under the hay loft was the pony stable, later to become the garage for the car, and under the chaffing loft the chaff house. Parting the barn floor from the bays were two timbered divisions about 3 foot 6 inches high with a small door at the ends to let sheep in and out of the bays. Nailed to the top timber were leather strips at intervals for the shearers to park their shears either when they had shorn their sheep or in emergencies as in the case where a sheep does not approve of the way it is being treated and responds in the only way that it knows best to what it considers its ill treatment.

A little way off was a French barn for further hay and corn storage. These buildings allowed us to almost double the number of livestock that we could house as compared to the old farm, with two

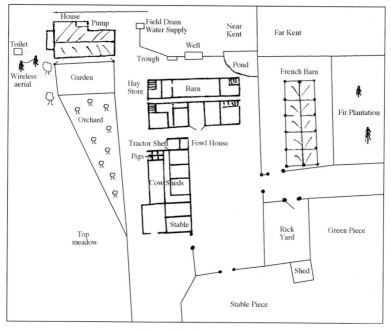

Plan of the farm layout

11

Chaff cutter

stables instead of one, and three cow houses. One great advantage was the fact that with the exception of one cattle shed every animal could be fed without moving out from under the roof in very wet or cold weather, another that the arrangement made for far easier cleaning out of the stables and cow houses.

In the barn was an engine which drove the chaff cutter on an upstairs level, the two being linked by an endless belt that passed through a hole knocked in the wall. A little planning had gone into this arrangement to allow the same belt to reach and drive the threshing drum standing on the barn floor, which incidentally was paved by better flags than some of those in the house.

I shall never forget the first time that that engine—OUR engine—was started. The sheaves to be 'chaffed' were placed ready on the loft behind the cutter. The belt was placed on the pulley of the engine and the chaff cutter by our waggoner, Bob Williams (then in his fourth year working for us), who then put in the required amount of petrol (or so we thought) into the carburettor, engaged the starting handle and the primer petrol was sucked in. Pop pop poppop it went—'music to mine ear', as the poet said. The wheels turned faster and faster, but then it started to slow down and there was an almighty BANG. I'm sure my heart stopped and that I

Winnower

jumped a yard in the air, but to crown it all the chaff cutter was going backwards! Slowly it all came to a halt.

Bob figuratively took his cap off and scratched his head. 'Thought the belt was a bit slack,' he said. 'Shall have to put a twist in it.'

This initially sounded daft to me, but then the penny dropped. (When a driving belt is placed on the pulleys of the driver and the driven in parallel both will turn in the same direction, in this instance clockwise, which was forward for the driver, the engine, but for the chaff cutter this was backward. To correct this, when the driving belt is placed on the second pulley the belt is given a half turn, so that the driven is now turning in the opposite direction to the driver, the engine. This is generally termed a 'crossed' belt.) No sooner said than done and a trial turn of the engine, which I watched with some trepidation, proved the point without another big bang.

'We'll try using more petrol to warm it up before it goes on to paraffin.' So we did.

Primed with petrol, the carburettor was filled again and once more the starting handle was swung—pop pop pop poppop. The waggoner stood by armed with a bottle of petrol feeding the carburettor as he thought necessary, but I had cleared out for I couldn't see him for smoke and was waiting for the next explosion. It didn't come and gradually the smoke started clearing. That pop pop pop of the engine and the crunch, crunch, crunch of the blades of the chaff cutter cutting the sheaves into chaff were lovely sounds. We cut more chaff in the next ten minutes than we would have done in an hour by hand and I realised that with any decent luck I should never again have to sweat turning a chaff cutter. The chaff fell through a chute to the floor below from where it had to be carried to the stable, usually in a very large sack, where it was placed in a large barrel that had the one end taken out. A couple of buckets of water was added and mixed with the chaff to soak, so making it more easy for the horses to eat and digest and so provide more time in the day for work.

The engine, a 5 H.P. Petter, was water-cooled and could be used for several hours without any fear of overheating. However, for safety reasons the engine had to be enclosed in a room of its own and this was achieved by partitioning off a portion of one of the bays with corrugated sheets.

A winnowing machine and the threshing drum stood on the barn floor. The latter had a very heavy wooden frame so as to remain stationary when the drum was being run at speed, inside which was mounted what was more or less a skeleton drum with lateral bars, and this in turn was mounted on a heavy spindle that extended beyond the frame and on which was mounted a pulley for the driving belt. The drum arrangement turned at high speed inside a cage that enclosed half the circumference of the drum, the open half giving access to a slot in the frame where the un-threshed corn was fed. Once threshed the seed and small stuff was forced through the cage behind the drum whilst the straw was carried on beyond the cage where it dropped onto the floor completely denuded of seed. One man put sheaves from the one bay to the feeder and another took away the threshed straw and placed it in the other bay of the barn for feeding or bedding at a later date. This system was ten times the speed of the old method with the flail or 'threshal', the only drawback being the resulting mixture of grain and chaff. This was raked out into a heap to the one side of the barn floor and then had to be winnowed. We fed this mixture into the winnower where it fell on to riddles which were being continually shaken from side to side in the stream of wind generated by the large fan—one of the most boring jobs on the farm, if not on earth, and not always the most pleasant either. Whilst it was usually done in wet or very cold weather and you were at least sheltered and warm from the work, against this was the dust, dust and more dust. Shut the doors, open the doors, shut some and open others—and it's still there. Meanwhile the fan pulled in cold air in over your hands, and being driven through a gear and shaker by a crank arrangement, made a sound that translated into 'Twice eleven is twenty two, Twice eleven –' on and on and on. Once you started hearing it there was no stopping.

The primary use of the barn was, of course, the storage of unthreshed corn for feeding or threshing, but once the storage areas or bays were empty it had a secondary use for shearing and general routine processes which sheep require. In the early days the shearing was quite an occasion, neighbours banding together to help each other so that each farm's shearing was done in two or three days and was a companionable thing that added a little change to the daily routine. The womenfolk vied with one another as to the best dinner and tea.

The shearing benches, about 18 inches high, were placed on each side of the barn and had pieces of old leather strap nailed on the flat top in which to park the shears when they were not being used. A catcher would collect the sheep, whilst someone else rolled the fleeces ready for storage. As soon as a fleece was off the sheep this person would gather it up and place it with the newly cut wool downwards on to a flat, clean surface. The wool was closed together and the sides then turned in, when it would be rolled tightly from the tail end of the fleece towards the neck which was stretched and twisted to form a band and wound around the fleece in much the same way as a sheaf of corn. There was no clatter or noise, just an occasional bleat of a lamb or sheep, the continual 'clish, clish, clish' of the shears, and the varied chatter concerning markets, weather, and crops together with the occasional threats to a restless animal as to what the shearer would do if it didn't stay quiet —threats which were never carried out.

As a lad I was given a pair of shears and a lamb to shear. I had seen hundreds of sheep shorn, but that didn't make it any easier. The quips were endless. 'Do you think you will be able to finish it by dinner time?' 'Shall we bring the poor thing some grass?' Then

'Dunna thee [Radnorish for 'Don't You'] take any notice of 'em boy, they ain't much better than thee now, an' they bin at it for years'.

Such good-natured banter characterised this sort of activity and often made light of many an unpleasant job. It was to come to an end with the purchase of a house lighting plant, as its petrol motor was admirably suited for working a shearing machine with a few things added and others taken away, and a coupling contrived for the shearing head. One man could then shear as many as four men with hand shears. However, the noise of the engines made conversation impossible and sadly the magnificent dinners and teas provided by the housewife were also gone forever. You win some, you lose some.

In the barn there were a few pieces of graffiti that were both serious and amusing. In one place the dates for finishing the corn harvest were recorded, two from the 1890s recording the completion of disastrous harvests in November. Another gave the dates for certain incidents that were obviously recorded by a rejected suitor. Epistles had been scribbled on the boarding in the chaff room, and two remain in my memory: 'Oh Lord, look in Mercy upon me, for the sorrows that burden my soul', and 'I've one thing to say about drinking, just now it 'as entered my 'ead, if I dunna drink w'en I'm livin, for sure I can't w'en I'm dead'. There were quite a few more that were unreadable on account of age or spelling but I have always wondered what was written there.

When we acquired it, the farm was run down. The previous farmer had had no children, and so lacked the extra manpower needed to run the farm well. Also lacking capital to invest, the buildings, hedges, gates and land deteriorated, a sad end to a lifetime of effort and labour. Nevertheless, it had always been reckoned as a 'good' farm by people on the outside looking in and, because of its state, my father managed to acquire it at what could be considered a 'knock down' price. This engendered a certain amount of envy at a later date when success was apparent.

As often is the case in this area the cultivatable land was in the region of half of the acreage, with the other half woodland and rough grazing. This meant that the main income was derived from the one half, the poorer half providing the living for the parent stock at certain times of the year and timber for fencing and general maintenance. The farm had a quarter of a mile of private road from the house to the council maintained road, which in this area is a very short farm road, except when a start is made to re-surface it, and then it becomes a mighty long way! So there was also a need for stone, and there was a quarry near the highest point on the farm, though the stone was so hard as to be reckoned too hard for general road making. In fact it was the hardest stone known in the vicinity and had been quarried when the road to Abbey-cwm-hir was made in the 19th century by the owner of the Abbey-cwm-hir estate. I am told that my grandfather was one who then worked in this quarry.

There was always water in the bottom of the quarry which in the springtime held tadpoles and newts by the dozen, and was the scene of many happy hours of play. On the steep slope below there was water-washed gravel and even a sand pit where the rabbits dug their burrows, and below that again a rock quarry of soft rock suitable for farm roads, as with a cover of sand or gravel it provided a fair road for farm vehicles.

One day we were 'Rising rock' from the quarry on the side of the council road ready for use on the farm. A large block was being worked upon and my father said to my brother and I, 'You two, get well out of the way and I'll get that wedge out that's holding that lot up, so that if it does come suddenly there'll be only one to get out of the way, and you two have a lot more to lose than me'.

My father had only struck about two blows when a huge patch of rockface came loose and started a veritable avalanche. He turned and ran down the steep rockface followed by this huge wave of rock and seemed to disappear below it. The noise was like that of growling thunder, with dust everywhere. For a split second I thought that he had had it, but his momentum had carried him right across the road and into the hedge and a haven on the other side. Did he have some doubt as to the safety of what he was about to do? Or was it a light-hearted joke, because if it was it nearly turned sour. It took us all the rest of that day to clear the road.

The farm was also well provided for with water. Three-quarters of the farm boundary was marked by watercourses, and a stream running more or less through the centre meant that there were few 'dry' fields, one of these being the Bottom Meadow where there was an outcrop of stone that resembled concrete.

The main stream was the river Clwedog that ran from north to south almost parallel with the road to Abbey-cwm-hir, and which more or less formed the western boundary of the farm. Its meandering course over a fairly sharp fall, meant that the water ran fast in places and slow in others. In the latter the finer sand was gradually deposited and accumulated which we used in mortar, the coarser sand in concrete. After a heavy flood there was always a harvest of sands for all purposes, strangely enough the same amount of each type arriving and never seemed to get any less.

The south-east border was marked by Pandy brook, always referred to as just Pandy. A small stream, this had its source quite close to Beddugre and meandered south-westwards until it joined the Clwedog shortly after passing the extreme southern point of the farm. It flowed over soft rock and clay which in some places formed 'heaves' of blue clay in mid-stream. If you pushed a stick about 10 or 11 feet long straight down into one of these heaves until only the brushy top was showing, in a week or so it would have completely disappeared, having sunk further and further into the depths from which this clay was coming. They came and went—as one disappeared another seemed to appear, not necessarily close by but there were always one or two about in the distance of half a mile or so.

In one way they were quite useful. Often in the late spring and summer blow flies laid their eggs in the wool of any sheep or lamb that had dirtied itself. The animal had to be caught and the eggs, or possibly maggots by then, had to be got rid of before any serious damage was done to the sheep—if allowed to go un-treated the maggots would eventually cause the sheep to die a horrible death.

The then treatment was a disinfectant lotion having a base of carbolic acid diluted and mixed with other ingredients, a mixture which stank to high heaven. But the soft blue clay acted as a soap. If well rubbed over smelly hands and then washed off, which took some doing, the hands were a lot more pleasant to live with. Even so one was reluctant to put the fingers in the mouth to give long distance whistle commands to the sheepdog.

Beddugre, or The Giant's Grave, is a huge mound that as far as I know has never been investigated. The reason is supposed to be that anyone approaching for this purpose is met with a violent thunderstorm, but whether there is any truth in this I leave for others to decide. The Giant's Grave was as good an indicator as to what the weather was going to be for the next day or so as the barometer. In the summer, if the day was fine and likely to stay that way, cattle would climb up on the mound and after having grazed for a while, lie down there to chew their cud. In winter, if the sheep were seen

Beddugre stands out on the horizon.
Pandy rises just to the left of the picture

to be coming down from the hill on the edge of night, as we say, it would portend a stormy night—nature giving them pre-knowledge of something that us human beings have lost. If at the same time the Brecon Beacons, away to the south, looked a 'bad colour' then it was sensible to bring the sheep to where you could find them if it should snow very heavily and cover them.

From Beddugre, Pandy soon forms the boundary of a small farm which has the name of New House. This must be one of the oldest New Houses in Radnorshire for it is believed to have been built in the 17th century, and once formed part of a small community of which only three properties remain, all to the south-east of the stream.

Just inside the eastern boundary was a part of the farm where something happened many years ago that would not be possible at the present time. The boundary itself was marked by a small stream that entered Pandy just outside the farm boundary, and along which ran a wire fence. By its nature the fence did not run in a straight line and so was difficult to keep in good repair, with wires becoming slack and allowing sheep to stray. As both farms on each side of the stream were absolutely devoid of shade, an agreement was reached that was supposed to improve the situation for both farmers. This entailed moving the fence towards the east, taking 20 yards of land from the neighbour's farm, in return for which the then owners of our farm were to plant a shelter belt on the strip of land so 'acquired'. Sad to say the trees were not planted. Thus one farm lost a couple of acres or thereabouts and the other gained it by what proved to be purely false pretences.

One field in particular by the Pandy was quite steep. One morning, when taking a load of fencing material to the bottom of this field, I decided to take the field at a tangent because there had been a frost overnight and a slight thaw was taking place. To my horror the load started to push the tractor and similar to correcting a skid on a car, I steered in the direction of the skid only to find that the tractor, the trailer and me—I had no choice after all—were going sideways straight down the bank, with the one wheel of the tractor turning forwards and the other backwards. Not to be undertaken if you have a weak heart. Suffice it to say that the tractor and trailer was left where they stopped until later in the day when the soil had thawed out completely.

CHAPTER II
School and Early Days

Changing school was for me quite a traumatic experience. My brother would stand up and fight, and could he! He was taller than me, more slender, very quick on the turn, whereas I was none of these and suffered accordingly. But I also had no wish to fight, I saw it as a waste of strength and rather useless, and only fought as a last resort, and so was dubbed a coward. But I was content to be left alone to read and think.

There was one place I could always win and that was at my desk, which invariably led to trouble in the schoolyard. A lot of heartache can be caused without a blow being struck. 'Oh. We forgot about you, the best thing is for you to keep goal'. Or 'You will have to go pairs with so and so', a perfectly useless partner to make it sure that you lost. There's no-one more cruel than jealous children, but as I preserved my ego in school, that unfortunately fuelled the fire.

Whilst new friends were made, I was not the best at doing this.

Another problem was convincing the new headmaster that at nine, going on ten years of age I was in the Seniors and Standard Four in the previous school. Things were a little different then to the present. The school catered for all ages from five to 14, the then school leaving age. The child concerned 'officially' left school at the end of the term when this magnificent age was attained, but it was more usual that as 14 was approached, attendance declined as the pupil was considered well enough educated by the parents and more value at home than in school.

The school was divided into three sections: Infants, Juniors and Seniors.

Infants covered from five to seven or eight when children moved to the Juniors, then on to the Seniors at age ten to prepare them for that almighty obstacle the Eleven Plus. Although few were able to take advantage it was a mark of the ability of the school as to what percentage of pupils passed this exam.

The Infants were divided into the First Class, Second Class, and Third Class, and it was this class that passed into the Juniors, who were divided into Standard One, Two and Three. Due to my age and date of my birthday I should have been at best in Standard Three in the Junior Class. Claiming to be in Standard Four was putting myself in the Seniors and the general feeling was that I had no right there, gaining neither the approval of the headmaster nor the rest of the class for that matter. Eventually I was put in the lowest position in the Seniors where I had to prove the truth or otherwise of my claim. Suffice it to say that at the end of the term, I had moved up the class order.

One advantage of the new school was that it was a mile closer to home than before, but the way was still largely across fields, some of which was the rough land of the Rhos. The route was shorter in summer, when a more direct route through some bogs could be taken. An hour was usually ample time to get there, except maybe in the winter with snow on the ground.

When we each reached the age of 12 we were thought responsible enough to ride bicycles, I enjoying this trust, therefore, two years after my brother. We were bought second-hand ladies bicycles, and though the distance by road was considerably more than that on foot, the time taken for the journey was much less. With my bicycle I was given strict instructions: 'You follow your brother and keep nearer the side of the road as well'.

This had a sequel. One frosty morning, after passing over a small stone bridge where the sun did not reach until later in the day, my brother stood up on the pedals so as to better tackle the sharp incline. Not to be left behind I followed suit. He promptly skidded and fell right across in front of me, leaving me no chance to stop or swerve and I rode over his neck, my right-hand pedal making a nasty gash in the back of his head, which bled freely. My brother refused to return home, and further on we passed the coalman on his way to deliver a load of coal to the farm. He reported to our parents that he had seen us going to school and the one had got a handkerchief covered in blood around his neck! At school First Aid was administered by the headmaster in the guise of iodine which he poured into

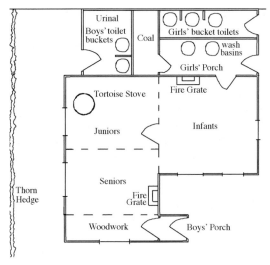

Boys' toilet buckets — Urinal — Coal — Girls' bucket toilets — wash basins — Girls' Porch — Tortoise Stove — Fire Grate — Juniors — Infants — Seniors — Thorn Hedge — Fire Grate — Woodwork — Boys' Porch

*Drawing illustrating the layout of
Llandewi village school*

the wound and smoothed the flap of cut skin back down. A pair of very anxious parents awaited our return from school, and my brother carried the mark for life.

The new school was shaped like a letter L in reverse, with the Senior and Junior classrooms in the vertical, and the Infants and the girls' porch in the base. The playground was formed of gravel, no doubt sieved from the nearby river Ithon and trodden to a concrete-like surface by generations of small boots.

At the base of the inverted L were the utilities, added on almost as if an afterthought. Extremely basic, the 'Boys' contained a trough and two cubicles with galvanised buckets under hinged lids with the necessary seating arrangements. There were never any fasteners or latches on the doors in my time.

To satisfy the proprieties of the day the 'Girls' was approached by a pathway on the other side of the building and here there was a little consideration to the niceties in as much that they had two washbasins with a cold water tap over them, and a door leading to the toilets. We called these facilities 'porches', and the boys' was furnished with wooden strips placed horizontally at varying heights on which coat hooks were fixed that showed signs of once having numbers.

The girls' porch's water supply came from a spring via a brick reservoir on the slopes of the Gaer, which gave rise to a fairly high water pressure. As every boy will know, a finger held on the outlet of a tap will cause the water to spray in any desired direction, and the temptation was too great. The door from the Infants' classroom opened into the girls' porch and in summer boys would often wait for the door to open—and Hey Presto. One day one of the boys—

Llandewi village in the 1930s with the Gaer in the background. The school building is that with the long uninterrupted roof just to the left of centre

I plead not guilty—decided to do a really good job of it, but was unaware that the schoolmistress realised what was happening and had decided to take a hand in the proceedings. Instead of opening the door slowly as the girls would have done, she did it quickly so as to get a good view of the perpetrator, but instead got an eyeful of water. There was no need to sound the retreat, it was automatic and rapid.

Up to this time we were free at any time to go to the girl's porch if we needed a drink of water and the way we abused the privilege rebounded on our own heads when the girl's porch was pronounced 'Out of Bounds' and we were given a couple of stripes each with the cane, and two hundred lines to be written after school before we could go home. A piece of school paper was folded into the books that we were using for the next lessons and any moments when the headmaster turned his back or was looking elsewhere a few lines would be written on the hidden piece of paper and the normal writing resumed when again under observation:

I must not spray water from the taps,

I must ——; half of them were written during lesson.

The punishment was accepted without question, but with the girls' porch strictly out of bounds it meant eating dry sandwiches on a hot summer day, and having no refreshment after playing football for three-quarters of an hour. We had to find an alternative water supply.

The one source of water open to us was the village pump (supplied from the same spring), which we could reach by going through the churchyard. Deciding on a military style operation, we formed up in ranks in the schoolyard, with a few exceptions, as there always is, and at a word of command marched through the churchyard in single file where everyone had a drink, if only a token one, and marched back into the schoolyard singing the old adage:

> At the pump, At the pump
> where I first got Drunk
> And the Bobby came and hobbled me away,
> He caught me by the collar
> And he made me pay a Dollar,
> and now I am happy all the day.

which was sung to a well known hymn tune. Then we all re-formed in ranks and dismissed.

The 'Out of Bounds' order was rescinded forthwith, and in return we abstained from giving the girls their previous water treatment.

Another incident that could have been poached from Richmal Crompton's *Just William* books and which I view with mixed feelings: was it an ingenious ruse, a triumph, a real deceit or was it just the schoolboy's rebellion against school discipline?

Our headmaster had three children, two boys in the County School and a daughter who sat in front of me in class. (To give the headmaster credit, he never once to my knowledge showed any favouritism toward her.) One day the County School in Llandrindod Wells had to be closed due to an infection called 'the Itch' which was caused by a microbe that burrowed beneath the skin, mostly in the area of the hands and wrists, notably between the fingers where they joined the hands.

For once I had a brainwave. I told my cousin, who also shared my desk, that as I sat close to the master's daughter who was in contact with the itch at home I would be the most likely to catch it—and this I would pretend to have happened. I started to rub the backs of my hands as if they were itching, and scratched a little between my fingers. Next morning he started doing the same. We tried not to make it too obvious, but to make it look as if we didn't want anyone to see, but at the same time making sure that they did! On the following morning we asked a couple of reliable friends to join in as reinforcements, but made it a condition that they were not to get too enthusiastic as that could cause the whole scheme to blow up in our faces. We also had to ensure that we kept the scheme from a couple of 'teacher's pets'—not his daughter I hasten to add—at all cost.

All went according to plan and the district nurse was called, by which time our fingers were slightly reddened by our rubbing and scratching. We sat for two hours rubbing and scratching, waiting to see what decision would be made, whilst we were treated to full instructions as to making and using sulphur ointment, together with a detailed routine for washing frequently and using towels of our own. It was as long as any two hours that I ever remember, but finally we were told the school would be closed and we should report back a week later. Best of all we did not have to tell any lies at home, simply that the school was closed for a week on account of the itch.

They say that Satan looks after his own, so believe it or not there were two genuine cases before the week was up, giving our scheme full credibility, but our parents were never told the real reason as to how that closure came about.

The visits of the school dentist were dreaded. He arrived armed with an adjustable chair, a bottle of cocaine, a syringe, some tablets with which to make some pink water to 'wash away' the aftereffects of his work—and a pair of diabolical pliers. What a setting for a nightmare, and this one did not go away.

The first time he came he didn't take out any teeth, he just sat you in the chair, asked you to open wide, looked into your mouth and made such remarks as 'Hm', 'Ha', and 'Yes'. Taking out a little mirror on a handle, he then prodded here and there and finished by saying 'See you next week'. Generally that day was not too bad as discipline was somewhat relaxed on account of one person or another being called for inspection, as far as I remember in alphabetical order and therefore from whichever class they were in.

A form for a parent to sign giving permission for the resultant treatment, and giving the parent the option to be present, was given to you to take home and return with the relevant information. A few parents with maybe only one child would prefer to take their child for private treatment, but with the four of us it was too expensive, and money was at a premium anyway.

Being more or less the middle letter in the alphabet, my treatment would be near or about the middle of the day of the second visitation, not a very nice prospect for dinner time. The chair was set up in the centre of the Infants' room, that being the nearest place

26

School photo in 1932. The author is top right, his brother Jack in the centre of the back row, his youngest sister is in the centre of the front row and to her left is his oldest sister. Mr Lane, the headmaster, stands on the left

to running water in the girls' cloakroom, water that had to be heated in cast iron kettles over the open coal fire. The school rooms were rearranged so that all could go in and out of the building without going through the 'surgery', or the Torture Chamber as we decided to name it.

There was no need to tell the children not to talk, the desire to do so was lacking and there seemed to be nothing to talk about anyway. Thoughts were totally occupied on wondering when their parent would put in an appearance and what would follow. It is strange when you dread and hate the sight of your mother because of the consequences, yet I also felt for the poor beggars whose mothers did not bother to come; make no mistake there were some.

There was only a flimsy partition between the Torture Chamber and the adjacent classrooms. You saw the children going in, you heard their cries and no-one ever seemed to come out! The unwanted moment finally came once Mother arrived, and we prepared for the worst.

'George Lewis, please'.

Please, my foot. My heart sank but what was the point—half an hour with a bit of luck and it would all be over. The nurse held the door open for me, and that is something that I was not used to, for I always opened my own doors. It is funny how in moments of stress such little things stick in the memory when things I want to remember play hide and seek. That chair, how well I remember it, standing four square in the centre of the room dominating all.

Once ensconced in the chair I was treated with a cold, wet water-proof 'bib' that reached down and over my bare knees.

'Open wide', and the torture began. First the injections, with needles seeming to be stuck in all over the place, then I sat down in another chair whilst my brother and sisters were dealt with in the same way. Then it was back to the big chair, fearful of what was going to happen to you, with lips and tongue all funny, unable to answer questions properly, and then the dreaded moment. A big man with funnily-shaped pliers came and stood in front of you, like some ogre in a dream, yet you couldn't wish this ogre away.

'Open up'. The nurse stood behind the chair and put her hands on my forehead, they were nice and cool and made me feel better, while the Ogre got a grip on the offending molar, and with a wrench and a crunch said 'Hm'—that was number one, 'Ha, yes' as number two was extracted, and 'Yes' for number three. As each came out it was dropped into a bucket with a little plop. Silly, maybe, but I wondered what he would have said if there had been five or six to come out. Would his vocabulary have coped?

Some of the pink water was offered and I was told to 'Wash away'. The bucket of mixed teeth, red water and blood was held up for you to spit out the wash into. But you cannot spit properly, and the wash and blood drooled all down my chin on to the bib, was wiped up by the nurse, the fairy godmother in all this, who then helped me from the chair. I went outside, out of sight, and used the ample hankies that Mother had brought for us, and waited for the rest of the family to have their medicine.

These were milk teeth that were extracted, for it was considered important to get them out of the way so as to allow free and unhindered growth of the next set.

The district nurse, she who was so helpful during the travails with the dentist, also had the not too pleasant job of going through the children's hair to see if there were head lice (referred to as Boogies at our school) present, and if so give advice as to treatment. Often the lice would linger on one person who then had to be ordered to the local clinic for the treatment that apparently was lacking at home. This order had a double effect in as much that the treatment was effective, whilst the disgrace of having the children sent to the clinic ensured suitable treatment at home in the future. The joke that went round the school was that at the clinic they held the child's head under water until the lice were drowned.

Early October was conker time. Growing in the roadside hedge near the school was a conker tree, it and the nearby hedge being the subject of depredation by 60 children each year. It was strictly forbidden to climb the tree itself, as apparently some years before my advent a boy had fallen out of the tree while trying to reach conkers. During the 15 minute playtime the headmaster used to go into his house adjacent to the school for between five and ten minutes for a cup of tea, and his dining room and kitchen were at the back of the house out of sight of the forbidden tree. One day I and my cousin waited until he had disappeared, and like monkeys were up the chestnut so as to grab the higher up conkers (those being the only ones left). Imagine our dismay when the headmaster, instead of staying in the house for his usual five minutes or so, returned straight to the school where we would be in full view if we tried to get down.

Our only chance was to stay up where the foliage was thick and wait for the call into class, hoping that he would then be too intent on getting order to enable us to scramble down the tree on the blind side and so onto the road, creep around the outside of the school hedge until we were at the far end of the buildings, then climb the hedge, a thorn hedge at that, and pretend that we had not immediately heard the whistle calling us into class. Desperate situations call for desperate action and that was what the thorn hedge required—but if it had been a monkey-puzzle we would have climbed it. Off came our two jackets which were thrown on top of the trimmed thorns. Me being the smallest helped my cousin over, then he reached as far over and down as possible and yes—we were both across. Jackets back on, we made a noisy dash into school with our ready made excuse. 'We were up around and didn't hear the whistle, sir'.

Success, but we kept our rather scratched hands out of sight as much as possible. Those conkers, meanwhile, stayed up there till they fell down of their own accord.

The school, school house, playground and the schoolmaster's garden were all in the same enclosure, the garden actually being a strip separated from the playground with a netting and post fence. As is the case with all fences an occasional post rotted away at ground level, and when an occasion arose where one needed replacing I had an idea.

When the woodwork class came round on Thursday afternoon, knowing that our headmaster hadn't a clue as to how to replace a post but had one ready for the purpose, I volunteered to replace it for him. He jumped at the chance and I said I would like to have my best mate to help me. He agreed, but told us that under no circumstances were we to over exert ourselves—as if that were likely!

During the first 'lesson' we dug the old stump out—good, easy digging but nothing said on that score, quite the opposite in fact. Next Thursday, 'Please sir, can we finish our fencing job?'

'Oh yes, certainly'.

One disgruntled classmate chipped in. 'Please sir, shouldn't someone else have a chance?'

'No, when someone starts a job he should have to finish it'.

We deliberately put the post in about a foot out of line and went to the master to apologise and ask if we could put it right next week. 'Oh yes, if you think it is not good enough'.

Thus we had three afternoons of absolute freedom to do a simple job that should have been done in one. The master, my pal and myself were thoroughly satisfied, whilst the rest of the woodwork class were as jealous as blazes.

The river ran near the school and not far away a fence had been strung across it to prevent stock straying. This consisted of a strong wire cable from which was suspended what resembled a paling fence, made in sections about 6 feet long and with the pales facing upstream and the horizontal crossbars on the down side. As the water level rose the paling more or less floated on the water, anchored of course by the wire cable.

One school lunchtime there was quite a heavy flood and we decided to investigate this fence, but from the other side of the river, crossing by the bridge half a mile away. My brother (always the leader and me the follower) together with a few classmates set off, and as always when there is something interesting going on, time flew. We were just about level with the fence when the cry goes up 'We shall be late'.

It being half a mile to the bridge, a good quarter from the bridge to school, it was physically impossible to return in time by the way we had come. My brother, my cousin and I decided to chance the weir, as it was called—but the pales were nearly horizontal on the water. Holding on to the cable with both hands, my brother put his toes between the pales of the first section and the middle of each foot on the cross rail. This was fine in theory, but the moment his weight was transferred the foothold disappeared under the water. As each pale sank into the water, it meant an awkward reach to transfer to the next one which was still riding high. In the middle of the river, where the water ran fastest, holding on with two hands to the wire rope, keeping the left foot on the lower gate against the flow of water and getting the right foot into position on the higher gate became a balancing and contortion exercise of no mean proportions. Once on the middle section the force of the river was such that the pale remained almost horizontal and nearly on the same level as the wire cable; instead of the water going down past you, you appeared to be travelling upstream at a rate of knots! With my face at most a foot above the foaming water I was just a little frightened. But it was as far to go on as to go back, so I hung on, looked at the Gaer in the distance so as to reorientate myself, and truth to tell, said a little prayer. Eventually we gained the far bank, but there was no boasting of the feat, we were too glad to be on dry land once more.

We made the school in time, unlike our classmates who had run back across the bridge, but the episode was never mentioned in school or at home in case we should be denied access to the river, and that would have been a disaster of monumental proportions.

Everything in school revolved around time: time to go into school, time for dinner, time for play, and time to go home—this latter at a quarter to four. We would have preferred it to be a little earlier, so why not? No sooner said than done!

On cold or wet days the school was left open in play times and dinner time so that those who wished could go in for the sake of warmth. So one day we used the opportunity to push the school clock on five minutes, and went home five minutes early. The next day we got greedy, and pushed it on by 20 minutes. Come the adjusted time and the master looked at the clock. We waited with bated breath. 'Finish off your work', he said, the usual instruction for ending the school day.

Next morning the clock had been reset to the correct time and we waited for the axe to fall, the suspense was terrible. But it never

*Once a year we were regaled with a lecture on the evils of drink,
after which we had to write an essay on what we had been told.
A few of the better essays gained a certificate*

happened! Perhaps he thought that our anticipation of punishment
was enough to warn us not to do it again. But as a safeguard, for ever
after he consulted his gold watch which he wore on his Double

Albert. (On the other end he always carried a pair of folding scissors, used to cut any fingernails considered too long for school wear.)

Another similar incident occurred where I did not get away with it. When Headboy it was one of my duties to put out the protractors and rulers for geometry lessons. These were a very varied lot, some ancient and showing their age and ill use with just a few new ones to make up the number required. These were a nice yellow, practically un-marked and lovely and flexible and could be used quite effectively as a propellant for missiles of chewed-up paper formed into balls, much to the discomfort of the girls in the front row when the headmaster was looking elsewhere. This day I decided to have a little practice before the rest of the class arrived. As usual, good was not good enough and I gave a little extra bend to one of the new rulers for extra force, and the ruler fractured. I promptly dropped the broken ruler behind a row of seldom used books in the store cupboard and provided myself with another nice new yellow one.

When I took my place in my desk next morning I had a nasty shock to see the two halves of the broken ruler laid parallel in front of me. The message was clear, and sure enough as soon as the school assembled for the first lesson of the day it came audibly: 'George Lewis, would you please go out into the porch and wait for me'. And here is where he excelled, for the pupils inside were allotted their tasks while I received the first instalment of my punishment—waiting.

'Hold your hand out, please'. I received two of the best, and believe you me his best were pretty good but no worse than the ten minutes waiting for it. How he found out I have no idea.

My contribution at home during school days was to feed all the housed stock, which meant that I had to put the requisite amount of feed ready the previous night so as to make it quicker and easier in the morning. I had an absolute horror of being late for school, for I had hopes of staying on, but it proved to be an ambition never to be realised. On summer mornings I brought the cows in ready for milking.

After school it was whatever seasonal job was needed, for example hoeing swedes—thinning plants to growing distance. My father paid us one penny per row, long or short and the short rows were naturally done first. Later in the year there was help needed during the hay or grain harvest. If the field was near or on the way home, Mother would be there with our sandwiches and a jug of hot tea and as soon as that was disposed of, a pikel or a rake materialised almost from thin air for each of us and off you would go until 7 or 8 o'clock.

On Saturday and in the school holidays we also helped with any light work that was wanted, but Sunday was different. Only essential work was done, with the balance of the day being your own. It was on Sunday, therefore, that books came into their own, not farming books—I got enough of that in the practical sense—but books on wireless, and on engines and sources of power of any sort, even mill wheels and turbines. I found out about valve timing, angles of incidence and centres of gravity, voltages, anode and diodes, all with the intention of entering the R.A.F. My greatest helper in obtaining books was my Mother; at every church or jumble sale she bought all the books she could lay her hands on.

Another help during these years was music. Mother was a fairly competent organist, and many winter hours were spent with the whole family—Mother, Father, brother and three sisters—gathered around the harmonium. Father had taught sight reading before he and Mother started farming, so we had a fair start, but unfortunately

The school was in Llandewi, where the Price family lived. Ben Price is shown holding the telegram from the king on his mother's 100th birthday. Ann Price lived for a further two or three years

34

he had learned the Tonic Solfa method, so that at a later date we had to more or less re-learn to read the Staff. At times some of the neighbours would come over and then there would be a real singsong, at others we went to their places. Often these sessions ended with a cup of tea and cakes.

School continued much the same in summer as in winter except that it was cricket instead of football and that was not my strong point, I never was any good at swiping things with something else.

We had no official Football or Cricket Pitch but it was the custom to go and ask the farmer, Mr. Thomas of The Hall, for permission to play on the Ddole and he never refused us. Sometimes the grass was rather long, but then it was the same for both sides and we knew better than to grumble about it. The village pitch was more or less on the same patch except that it was wider and longer. For football we used poles with a cord strung between them instead of a crossbar. We were lucky to have 'Teddy Moseley' the postman who, if he had 'done his round' by our dinner break, would come and act as coach, giving us a head start when we came to play other schools. By the time I was 17 I was able to join the Llandewi men's team.

Our 'home' pitch at Llandewi was marked out to the requisite size with the aid of a bag or two of sawdust and a length of binder twine. When we travelled 'away' we always took the goal nets with us as our village was one of the few to possess a pair. On these journeys our 'team bus' was a covered wagon with driver loaned by the local grocer. Wooden egg boxes were placed along the sides and across the front and the goal nets laid down the centre, leaving the rear of the small lorry open except for the tailboard which stood about 18 inches high. At one village sports we won the competition which made us each the proud owner of a miniature cup and, as usual on such occasions, necessitated an adjournment to the local to have a drink. On the way home, one who had been very hard to persuade to leave the bar behind requested a stop but the driver declined. So when the lorry reached a steep hill which it had to climb, the plaintiff was propped up looking over the tailboard and proceeded with the business in hand. When the lorry turned a sharp corner he overbalanced, but fortunately fell sideways into the nets which broke his fall. Efforts to restore him to a more normal position proved awkward as by some means his head had gone through the mesh of the net and there seemed to be no way to get it out, even to the

The school football team in 1934. From left to right:
Back row: Jack Evans, Arthur Williams, Haydn Morgan,
Mansel Lewis
Front row: Tom Morgan, J. Lewis, George Lewis
With the exception of Jack Evans, all were related one way or another

more sober of us. To cut the net was absolutely unthinkable, and it took several miles before he was released.

On a different occasion, due to a draw, a match had to be replayed. The original field was no longer available due to farming needs and so a field used for grazing was the only venue open to us, each side battling equally with patches of tall grass and cowpats, one being used to serve for the penalty spot. At one point the game was disrupted when a rabbit was disturbed from its squat and both teams had five minutes chasing a completely bewildered beast.

One other momentous game comes to mind. It was toward the end of the season, but the weather was a shocker. When it wasn't raining it was hailing, and when it wasn't hailing it was sleeting, great big dabs and literally millions of them, so much so that the opposite goal disappeared from sight at times. But 'the show must go on', and go on it did, friend and foe appearing like spectres out of the gloom as the lines disappeared along with the spectators—including our one supporter. I cannot remember who won that game.

One really high spot in the football year was the ladies football match at Rhayader Carnival. This was played, or should I say fought, with as much verve and determination as ever was shown at a cup final. Feet and elbows became weapons of attack and the crowd of spectators got so excited that complete control was out of the question. Several stewards were recruited to try and keep the crowds off the patch so that the women could have enough space to play on, but even so they usually failed and the match would finish on a 20 yard wide strip between the goal posts.

After one of our own practice games, to avoid any danger from dehydration we adjourned to the Walsh Arms in Llandewi in preference to the village pump, where it was warmer and we could all sit down and rest our weary bones. As chance had it, a farmer arrived in his car that more often than not was a stock carrier rather than a personnel job, and true to form he had a load of weaner pigs on board. Just a quick one he said, but you know how it is, what with the chance and the time for a discussion, and discussion takes time and that quick one got longer and longer. It only ended when someone rushed in with the news that there was a little pig running up and down the road—the car door had burst open and allowed the little pigs to gain their freedom, only to get hopelessly lost and frightened.

'How many should there be?'

'Seven'.

It is not easy to catch a pig, especially after they have rummaged in dirt and mire and become slippery, coupled with the fact that in the outside gloom you could only see the beggars now and then. Finally, we thought, we had them surrounded and drove them into the pub yard and thence into the stable.

'I owe you a pint each', says the pig man, and then 'Oh, B—, there's only six here, Where the H– is that other little B–?'

To everybody's surprise the joker walks in, attracted by the sounds of his one time mates, was quickly surrounded and chaperoned in to join them where he gave a satisfied grunt as if to say 'Glad to see you again'.

Llandewi village shop was a place of 'delights and delectations', as Leonard Sachs would have said. Sweets by the jar but pennies were few! The only certain ones were on our birthday and at Llandewi Lamb Fair.

This small shop gradually became an extensive and profitable business, starting off with a delivery and collection service using horses and carts and progressing to quite a number of lorries and vans. In reality the shop became a façade for the warehouse which lay behind it, a warehouse used to store bulk produce for farmers and gardeners, as well as game, hares and rabbits awaiting transport to further afield. As there was quite often no-one around, a local chap decided he could make a nice little bit of cash by collecting a few rabbits from the warehouse and selling them over the counter in the shop. How often he managed it is not known and he's not telling either! It even became the official Egg Packing Centre during the Second World War for the whole of the county of Radnorshire.

The founder of this business, by the name of Nicholls, was, above all, a strict time keeper and expected his employees to be the same. The story is told that on one occasion one of his old and trusted employees arrived a few minutes after time to find his employer was at the door waiting for him. As he approached, Nicholls took out his pocket watch and held it in full view. The employee rolled up his

Llandewi Stores with the church beyond in the 1930s

sleeve to display his own wristwatch and remarked, 'I've got one of them Boss, and 'es a good 'un'. Nothing more was said.

Certain parcels were delivered to the shop, tied with metal bands around them that were rather difficult to break. Then someone had the brilliant idea of putting a 2lb weight under each band and cutting it with a hatchet designed to open wooden boxes, in the manner of a chisel and anvil. The process worked beautifully, until the weights and measures man arrived when there was a scramble to secrete the mutilated weight.

Away from school and on the farm we used to conjure up all sorts of games and activities. At one end of the range of farm building (see plan on p.11) was a stairway that led to our gymnasium and play room, in fact the granary with a wooden floor about twenty feet square. Some of the 'play' involved sorting out the potatoes which were dried there before putting into winter storage, at which point they needed sorting or, more appropriately, sizing. Large were kept for eating or sale, medium for planting next year's crop and smalls for feeding to the pigs. With two buckets placed 10 to 15 feet away the stage was set for a game similar to boules.

Ten potatoes each and Game on!

Even so, handling and grading each potato individually was a slow and extremely boring procedure, so it was decided to sieve them. Several sizes of netting were used around the farm and two were soon found to suit our purpose. Two square frames of equal size were made and a piece of netting of the required size nailed on each. Placing the larger of the two on the top of the other, this one would retain the larger or eating potatoes while the 'sets' or seed potatoes plus the smalls would fall through, they in turn continuing to fall to the floor through the second netting. The job was done in a quarter of the time leaving more time to play potato Boules!

For a while after the potatoes had been taken away to the winter store and the threshing had not yet being done the floor was clear of all obstructions and became our boxing ring, not that we had any proper boxing gloves. Instead we resorted to using thorn-proof hedging mittens, but with these we confined our punches to the body. Thereby hangs a story. A circus had come to Llandrindod Wells and one of the acts was a boxing Kangaroo. We decided to train Shep to become a boxing sheepdog, so on with the mittens and we played a bit rough with Shep. He soon cottoned on, and soon we had a good game going. As we had these thick gloves to protect our hands we got a bit hard and Shep responded in kind. The sequel was that every time we had to go to do a hedging job and Shep saw the mittens he went straight in to the attack and took a lot of persuading that it was business this time.

The animal housing structure had a lean-to which ended with the pigsty. In the early days the roof was covered with grey stone tiles, not slates, which were anchored over the rafters with oaken pegs, their weight alone ensuring that they wouldn't be blown away in a gale. I once managed to climb up onto the ridge of this roof where I started to imitate the stock cockerel, waving my arms and crowing to complete the impersonation. Carried away, I overbalanced, fortunately toppling towards the side where lay the midden, or mixen as we called it. I was no longer in control of my body, and down the roof I went, leaping to at least make sure of an upright landing which was the best that I could hope for—and achieved, coming to earth in the nice soft midden where I remained until my brother arrived. I was green with chagrin and annoyance, not to mention what else, whilst he laughed until the tears were rolling down his face. As for me, I had to bite my tongue, for knowing him as I did he would have left me to find my own way out rather than help extricate me.

The two quarries on the farm were just magnetic to us and a source of worry to our parents when they discovered that we had been climbing up their face with the possibility of a fall of a hundred feet on the menu. A ban was imposed.

At the top of the higher quarry, various larger stones that were too hard to break for use in repairing the roads were left lying around. Start them rolling down the wood with its slope of 45 degrees or greater, and their progress was spectacular until they hit a tree and came to a halt. Sometimes one would reach the road at the bottom of the hill, but this was rare and the traffic almost non-existent. One afternoon I found a 'beauty'—big and almost round. I started it down the wood just like a bowler does on the green, but as soon as it left my hand I heard the Post Office van coming. I could do nothing about it . They say that one's past life is sometimes seen in a split second, but I'll swear I saw my future. For once my fairy godmother looked graciously on me and the stone dropped on the road less than a yard behind that van, leaving a hole in the tarmac as deep as a good saucer. What it would have done to that van I leave you to judge, but I removed the stone far away to avoid any suspicion falling on it and me, and you can be sure that I never, ever rolled another stone down that wood.

Much of our relaxation was gained from catching rabbits and, occasionally, a hare. In this we used our constant companion, Shep, the sheepdog. Whilst the rabbits were likely to be out and about, we collected a bundle of bracken, stuffing bits a full arm's length into every entrance of a rabbit burrow, or bury, that we could find. Then Shep was sent off to find any rabbits which, we hoped, would make their way back hot foot to the burrow and home—as they thought. In they popped, but finding the way blocked, hesitated before trying to get back out. In their indecision they allowed us time to get there and capture the unfortunate animals. All the holes were carefully unblocked before we left, so that other inhabitants remained in ignorance so that they would become unsuspecting victims at our next visit.

Shep was a friend, a helper and a money-spinner. We were given Shep as a puppy, 'He's yours,' says Dad, 'do what you like with him'. Shep only had to be shown how to do something one day and he would do it the next. Once we taught him to climb a ladder, but we failed to encourage him down and so every time we had to climb up ourselves and bring him down. Eventually he became a little fed up with the game, caught me by the backside of my trousers and gave a little growl as if to say enough was enough. Soon he learnt to only climb where he knew it was possible to jump down easily.

Then there was the river—good for swimming, sailing boats and most of all for fishing. To most people that conjures up pictures of a man casting with a fly rod on a beautiful stretch of broad, slow flowing water, but our river was covered with trees and there wasn't room to swing a cat let alone a fly. On the basis of what you have you make use of, we found a hazel rod of about three years growth, nice and straight, (we soon had a little store of spares drying off in the granary in case of breakage), on which we fixed loops of wire at short intervals to carry the line from a cotton reel at the base of the rod. Hooks came from Selwyns in Llandrindod, thread from a ladies' jumper—very strong but a little thicker than we would have liked, and in place of gut we used a single strand of steel wire from a Bowden motorcycle control cable. We caught more trout with this kit than later when we could afford a more sophisticated outfit. We thought of the river as ours and we didn't see why we should pay for a licence for the privilege of fishing, so we never did. If any one approached us, we always took the precaution of hiding any fish that we had caught. As for Pandy, we sometimes fished this after dark with lights and spears specially made by the blacksmith—under sufferance, as making them was as much as his job was worth if he should be caught at it.

Where the field boundary fences ran up against Pandy there was often a pole across the stream from which a fence was 'hung' to prevent animals straying from one field to another. We often used to climb up on these poles and jump down on the other side, but on one of our fishing expeditions my brother did this and ended up in one of the clay heaves that abounded in this stream, and disappeared up to his waist. The heave acted almost like quicksand, with a vacuum underneath which was sucking him down. Luckily we were both wearing leather belts as well as braces, so one was fastened around the pole off which he had jumped for him to hold on to and to pull on, whilst I slipped the other belt under his arms and pulled on that. He came free, much to our relief.

It was winter time and by the time we had extricated him the fog had settled down thickly on to the ground, distorting both our lights and voices, shrouding us in total silence, as if an invisible blanket was all around. We went homewards as fast as we could go. thinking we knew the Rhos like the back of our hands—until we bumped into a stunted hawthorn bush that was way off where we thought we were. But the bush acted like a beacon to a sailor, it telling us that we were on one of the squatter's hedge banks and had been heading straight for one of the bogs. By now our trousers were frozen stiff, and when we fell into a gutter a few minutes later, we knew we hadn't far to go. Ten minutes later we were in the house with dry clothes on, my brother's soaked and clay clad trousers standing frozen and upright on the floor.

The mill pond at Llandewi was much loved by eels and trout, but they could have been in Timbuctu as far as we were concerned, for the simple reason that the mud was as deep as the water and we didn't dare to use a rod and line on account of being in full view of the village and the schoolmaster in particular. But one day the pond had to be drained to repair the sluice, for the water wastage was too great to keep the mill working for any length of time. Our chance appeared, for once the water was drained it just left a three foot channel running through the middle, where the imprisoned trout could clearly be seen.

These trout pushed upstream as far as they could go where the mud was not so deep, not much above our knees in fact and if you could keep moving you were okay. The knack was to grab a trout, one hand on its tail and the other over its gills and head, and then keep moving with it without floundering till dry land was reached. The strategy for the eels was somewhat different. Sometimes they failed to bury themselves completely and a couple of inches or maybe a loop stuck up out of the mud; this was grabbed, but no attempt was made to hold on to it, for instead you flung the eel to where others were waiting. Once an eel hit the ground, it would immediately start to head back to the water, for the direction of which they seemed to have an uncanny sense. This adventure had a very disappointing end, for both the trout and the eels tasted of mud, stale smelly mud at that, and were totally inedible.

In the warmth of summer we went to the river Clwedog, mostly on a Sunday, donned our bathing suits and beware all trout in less than three foot of water, for here we came—we knew every place where a trout would lie that could be captured. We each had our favourite haunts, and truthfully we caught more trout by 'groping' than we ever did with the rod and line.

During any heavy rainfall in October things would hot up. Out came the carbide lights, gaffs and spears—it was salmon time. Salmon returned to their spawning grounds as they had done for hundreds of years and they had been taken by the country people from the beginning of time. Illegal? Certainly, but what right had a body of men to say that these fish belonged to them whether in season or out. Anyway, the fish were on our patch, not theirs.

One year a weir was repaired downriver and built so high with no depth of water at the foot so that a good many fish threshed themselves to death in their attempts to get upstream. It was decided that this situation could not be tolerated and this gave rise to one of the last outings of Rebecca that took place in the area. A number of interested lads got together and with crowbars, pickaxes and iron bars destroyed the weir so that the water flowed freely and the salmon returned to their natural haunts and spawning grounds. It was widely reported at the time that explosives were used in its demolition, but don't ask me how I know it was different.

The weir was subsequently rebuilt with a shoddy pretence of a salmon ladder, but at least it did allow the salmon to reach their spawning grounds. The fact that it was still difficult for the salmon to find their way up the ladder resulted in a large number of frustrated salmon congregating there and gave the unscrupulous poachers a grand opportunity to make a big killing for profit, whereas people like us just had a fish or two for our own use.

Another Rebecca took place a few years later. A couple of our friends were caught poaching by the water bailiffs and were beaten up, one being knocked unconscious and requiring medical treatment. Involved in this incident was an officer of the law who was much disliked and had publicly stated that he would stamp out poaching, by whatever means it took. Rebecca was called out, and the 'Law' tempted. The message duly filtered through, 'They are on their way, get ready'.

What happened next we do not know, for the cars carrying the 'Law' got to within half a mile from flash point and then turned back. A spy? A favour returned? Who knows. Instead it was decided to give a massive demonstration of solidarity and for a short distance the river was fished clean of every possible fish which were then left lying on the river banks for all and sundry to see or take if they fancied one. Maybe it was wrong to take revenge on the fish, but we were incensed about the use of a baton with sufficient force to cause severe damage, and the *status quo* resumed.

Another pleasure was the shooting. As there was quite a large area of rough ground the game often included hares, pheasants and partridge each of which was worth shooting in terms of what we

Poachers gathering—The Rebecca

could sell them for. The uncertainty of what, if anything, got up was half of the pleasure. The poor humble rabbit, however, was different, for it took a really good shot in that rough to do better than one rabbit to two cartridges, meaning that the rabbit died in debt. So the method of control was snaring or netting with the use of ferrets, which someone in the valley kept for this purpose.

We had a gun each and if there had been a snowfall we would go out and have a bit of sport. I had not been allowed to use a twelve bore double barrelled gun until I was 16, and I remember quite clearly the first rabbit that I shot—I was too close and it was knocked about a bit. Part of the subconscious reason for being so close may have been due to the fact that if your first shot was a 'miss' you heard about it for the rest of your life. Even so, when I arrived home with my rabbit I had to run the gauntlet of comments like 'You're sure it was alive when you shot at it?' and 'Must have been suicidal'. But I had heard it all before and I was still proud of my rabbit.

There were two big dates on our calendar which we could count on: Knighton May Fair and the Sunday School Trip, the latter often to the Welsh coast. Knighton Fair took place on 17 May, unless that fell on a Sunday, and was where farmers went to hire a workman for the following year and tried to assess the likelihood of any boys on 'show'. When a prospective worker was seen he would be interviewed and if he seemed suitable would be given a shilling, called earnest money, as a token of being hired.

The story is told of a farmer of a pecunious nature who asked a prospective lad who was his previous boss. On being told, he said 'I'll 'ave a word wi' 'im and then I'll give thee thy earnest'.

Ten minutes later they met again and the farmer offered the shilling, saying 'Alright thee ca'st come, I got thee reputation'.

'Aye', says the boy, 'I met thy last year's boy and I ain't a-comin'.'

Abbey-cwm-hir was our nearest village, to which we used to walk on a regular basis. On one of our journeys home, my brother and I discovered a barrel of farm cider that had been left just through the gate of a farm entrance for the farmer to collect. Not being aware of the delivery, there it lay at our mercy. Not being out for blood, we would be content with a little drop, the problem being how to obtain it. The cork protruded from the bung hole by about a quarter of an inch and by tapping with a thin stone, plus a little persuasion from two pocket knives, one of which had a broken blade and beautifully served our purpose, the impossible was achieved and the cork succumbed. One difficulty remained, for which Mother Nature came to our assistance. There was a plentiful supply of dandelions nearby, from which we chose the longest and broke off the flower—but it didn't reach the cider in the barrel. So another was picked and inserted into the end of the first. Contact! Then came the next problem, when's enough enough? We decided to err on the side of caution, put the cork back in, hammered it in with a stone, and threw the incriminating dandelion stems and blossoms to float away down the river, while we floated happily up the road toward home.

This sounds like an almost idyllic childhood, once I had settled into the new school, but 1934 will always stay in my memory as the year when all my hopes and ambition were completely obliterated. Please do not mistake me, circumstances and not people were responsible for the situation. All in all my schooldays were good, if shorter than I would have wished.

The school leaving age was then 14, but at the age of 11 I earned and took my place at the top desk, a fact that automatically carried the honour of Captain of the Football and Cricket teams. Imagine when teams were being picked from 20 boys and the Captain was left until last! It was humiliating to say the least. Having this situation extended for three years through not being able to go to the County School rubbed salt into the wound. I kept my 'throne' until my last term in school, and only lost it then because as soon as you were 14 you unofficially left. On my last day I was tested by a schools inspector who promised to get me a scholarship. I lived on this hope for six months, but finally had to accept that it was not going to happen. I felt that my world was at an end, at least the world that I had hoped for.

CHAPTER III
Farming

The Thirties was a watershed in more ways than one. The price of farms were at their lowest, those for farm produce similar, partly due to the cheapness of imports, a situation aggravated by the business fraternity who favoured industrial development.

The move to a new farm meant a huge mortgage at a time when the future was uncertain, and must have been the subject of much worry and soul searching by my parents. How serious this was and how high the risk can be judged by the fact that the total income from the sale of animals and farm products for the year 1930-31 was £98. Against this was mortgage interest of £120, and a wages bill of £40, and we were a little deeper in debt at the end of the year than at the beginning. It was better for the seed and feed people to wait a while for their money than force the issue and get nothing, but nevertheless much needed animals which would have generated future income had to be sold to meet some of the bills.

Money was only spent on necessities that we could not grow ourselves—tea, sugar, maybe a pound of rice occasionally and a beef roast on special occasions. We would boil a fowl that had passed her sell-by date and been retired from the laying scene, and a rabbit or two that we had snared—cartridges being expensive—together with any casualty sheep (age immaterial) and of course the pigs, without which living was impossible to imagine, that is how pigs and farmers are such close friends. Vegetables were no problem unless there was a bad crop of potatoes and swedes; if the two failed then that was a disaster of a year's duration.

The new farm was suitable for producing beef and lamb, requiring forward planning of two years at the least and three realistically. That is the length of time it takes for a heifer to grow and produce her first calf, and generally speaking the offspring is not so good as from a mature animal—always assuming that all is well with the pregnancy, birth and provision of milk for the calf. Similarly with sheep. The mother had to be purchased or kept and fed for two years; a few ewe lambs in Radnorshire would have a lamb at one year old, but often at the expense of the mother who failed to have a lamb the following year and so is a loss instead of the hoped for gain.

We had immediate problems with stock bought at the farm's dispersal sale. One heifer bought to boost our cattle numbers slipped her calf and died as a result, a serious blow financially. An older work horse also bought at the take over sale became lame and more or less useless for some time.

The prospects were very bleak indeed and the living standard was, to say the least, low. Yet one bright spot as far as my parents were concerned was that at the time of our move my older brother was 12 years of age, which meant that in a couple of years he could leave school and replace one of the two hired hands. In a further two years I myself should be leaving school, and theoretically all help would then be provided by the family. At the time of the move I had appreciated what was in store for me, and hoped for a long time that I could move to a life that was not based on the farm. But when my last minute hoped-for scholarship failed to materialise, I had no sensible option but to work for my parents full time.

My brother took the place of the waggoner, who had come with us when we moved farm and was treated as one of the family. In exchange he was as loyal as they come, and would work during harvest-time until midnight or even later without a word of protest. In return he had days off when he wanted them, and as part of an unspoken gentleman's agreement this was neither abused or advantage taken either way. Around the time my brother reached the age of 14, the waggoner decided to get married and go and work on the Black and White long distance buses, an ambition of his. We decided to give him a decent wedding present and bought a Victorian mirror with a black enamelled frame decorated with flowers and festoons made out in gold. To test his reaction it was left in full view with nothing said, and react he did. 'Wherever did you get that monstrosity?' One defunct wedding present and bed linen was hastily substituted. It was always regarded as one of life's lucky escapes.

Two years after my brother had taken over the duties of the waggoner I took on the role of cowman, my father retaining responsibility for checking and feeding the sheep. The wage bill was replaced by a small cash allowance for each of us that made the purchase of harvest machinery possible. The old self deliverer, a corn cutting and sheafing machine which left the corn in sheaves to be tied with bands of straw taken from the sheaves as you worked along the row, a time consuming operation, was replaced with a binder which cut, sheaved and tied the corn—and didn't mind the thistles one little bit. Then, instead of threshing the corn in the barn with our own barn drum (threshing machine) and winnowed to remove the waste, the threshing was done by a contractor with a portable threshing machine in a couple of days, the corn stored in the granary and the threshed straw tied up in bundles and put in a rick to await the time when it was required for feeding animals. On the home front, as finances improved it became possible to have bread with jam and butter, as opposed to either one or the other. A little fresh meat also sometimes appeared on the menu.

Each day would start the same—banging on the wall of the bedroom early in the morning would signify getting up time, no matter what time you came home the night before. Actual getting up time was ruled by the sun with my father as his deputy, and he was just as compelling. That dance the night before was non-existent now; the cows and horses wanted their breakfast the same as any other day. (The only exceptions were Sundays, Good Friday—which was treated as a Sunday after the mid-day meal—and Christmas Day when only essential work was done after which it was a day of sport, shooting in our case.)

I would dress as fast I could before I had time to get cold and start to shiver.

Once downstairs it was into my wellies, and down to the buildings to feed the animals, keeping hands and blood moving, and in no time flat the cows and horses were tucking in to their breakfast with every sign of enjoyment. This was one of the pleasures and satisfactions of farming and keeping animals.

All farm animals have their individual character, and that provides much of the joy of farming stock. Despite common perceptions, sheep do each have their own personality, but because so many are kept together this often goes unnoticed unless their antics are really unusual. If one ewe that stays in mind should find herself at the rear of the drove when moving the flock, you would be wise to keep the dog at a slight distance, for if the dog went too close she would go berserk and only the best of hedges or fences would stop her. In one instance she managed to get through two wire fences—maybe not of the best quality but good enough for any ordinarily sensible animal—straight down a steep wood, over the bank on to the road which involved a drop of about ten feet, thence along the road on to a bridge with open work sides from where she plunged into the river in full flood, to become caught in a tree stump 20 yards downstream. She was rescued with a certain amount of damping of body and spirit—spiced with observations on sheep. This was an exceptional case, but a good shepherd will know the individual animals in a small flock, and many in a large one.

Ask any cowman and he will tell you that he knows each animal in his care, its potential as a milk producer, how it will react to any given situation, and its ability to hold its own with the other animals in the herd. Take Spotty, bought as a milk cow so as to allow the rest of the herd which were Herefords, not renowned for their milking capability, to pass on all their milk to their calves. Crudely described as a white cow with brown spots, she would stand quiet for you to milk her out in the field. She was slow to merge with the rest of the herd and started to produce less and less milk, and that which she did began to get a little yellow. In addition her clear white coat and skin became gradually more and more orange in colour. The vet was called and he decided that she was jaundiced for some reason or other, and gave her something to correct it. This worked for a while, but soon the milk was yellow again. One evening on going to collect the cows I found her on her side, her feet out from under her, head straight out in front, and unwilling to move. After some persuasion she was got on her feet, but acted like someone who has had one over the eight and had to be held up for some time to find her balance. By walking by her side and holding her up I managed to encourage her home. She looked as if she hadn't been grazing at all that day and her milk proved as yellow as a guinea. After further due consideration the vet declared that she was suffering from a nervous breakdown and nervous debility—in short, she was frightened to death of the other cows and it was affecting her severely.

We force fed her for a few days, drenching her with linseed gruel, but after a couple of days she would drink it out of the bucket with no trouble at all and started to fancy a little freshly mown grass. Her recovery was as dramatic as her illness, but for the rest of her days with us she was always pastured with the young stock and she never had a reoccurrence.

The day's activities would always be determined by how you found the stock in the morning, ailments needing immediate attention. One of the oldest diseases was liver fluke, the onset of which was very deceiving to the uninitiated. In the early stages the sheep put on weight and gave the impression that all was well or maybe very well indeed, for when the fluke is small and first enters the body it stimulates extra activity in the liver, in turn increasing appetite resulting in excessive fat being deposited, particularly in the abdominal cavity. The fluke parasite resembles a snail, only it is flat and almost an inch in length rather than rounded, and takes up residence in the bile ducts in the liver itself. If the infection is severe it will result in the sheep becoming severely debilitated and in due course its death if not discovered and treated in time.

This parasite has an amazing life cycle. The eggs of the fluke in the liver passed with the bile into the digestive system whence it was dropped on the ground with the animal's waste. From there it found its way by some means to the water snail which it used for an immediate host—it follows of course that wet land posed a greater risk for sheep than dry. The immature fluke stayed with its host until the following spring when it dropped off to climb up and attach itself to a blade of grass, which was then grazed and eaten by a foraging sheep. When it reached the stomach of the sheep it bored its way into the blood stream and was carried to the liver of the host where it bored its way into the bile ducts. Here it grew to maturity and laid its eggs to start the cycle all over again.

When fluke was discovered, nature was brought to the rescue. Every farmer had a flock of ducks and ducks loved the snails and so broke the cycle. But unfortunately a duck's legs are shorter than a sheep's so they cannot cover the same amount of land, and so couldn't provide a complete antidote—but they helped, and on the small farms were a great success. As a bonus they provided the housewife with a nice daily supply of duck eggs.

We had those ducks, 16 ducks and a drake all told. Mother told the story many times of once when the ducks were not laying and saying about it to our younger sister. She, with childish logic, replied, 'Maybe we should have drakes instead'.

During Double Summer Time the ducks' body clocks remained on G.M.T. and their time to arrive home to be shut in for the night remained dusk—or even slightly after if their clock only told them that it was time to go home when they were a long way away. This often meant that we had to 'wait up' to shut them in and keep them safe. But one night no ducks arrived and it was useless to look for them, as there was no way of knowing where they would be. Imagine the horror and dismay next morning to find 16 ducks and one drake dead and strewn over one of the fields near the house in varied stages of mutilation—the result of a visit from a playful fox. Gone was my mother's income from duck eggs and our insurance against Liver Fluke for over a year, as a fresh lot of eggs would have to be hatched and the ducks grow to reach maturity and laying.

Then, just prior to the outbreak of the Second World War, came the real killer—Australian Black Disease. In the morning the sheep would look well, but by midday one or two could be dead. The Ministry of Agriculture's veterinary service was contacted immediately if there was no other obvious cause of death, and a post mortem examination would reveal whether this disease was the cause.

One morning one ewe did not eat as usual and so we got on the phone to the vet, but tracking him down proved difficult. He had already gone to a farm at Penybont, the name of which we had never heard. Off we went to Penybont asking for 'Rhos Swydd Villa'. 'Not in Penybont' we were told. Then one spoke up, 'That's Sebastopol', and so it was. The nickname had stuck for so many years that it was just by chance that anyone remembered the original name at all!

The vet saw the ewe die and took blood and tissue samples from which a vaccine was made at Aberystwyth College. To complicate matters the ewe turned out to have quite a high concentration of liver fluke, so we divided our sheep into three equal groups and marked them accordingly. One group was given no treatment, the second injected with the newly made vaccine and the third given the vaccine and a dose of Liver Fluke medicine. There were no further losses in injected groups, but a number in the control group succumbed. The disease was thus positively identified, with all credit to the vet and the college.

While this disease was about only two other farmers said that they had lost sheep. Most asked us questions about the symptoms and treatment, but if asked whether they were losing sheep the answer was invariably 'No'. In which case I wanted to know why Boots the chemist sold out of Australian Black Disease Vaccine as quickly as they could get it? Such is farms and farmers.

It is not always possible to diagnose and treat these diseases. Taking the cows home one day, one cow started to cough and choke after going up a fairly steep bank. Thinking she was choking on something or other I forced her mouth open and put my hand down her throat as far as it would go but found no obstruction whatever, only for her to collapse and die there and then. Thinking that it was like shutting the stable door after the horse had bolted, I rang the vet who said, 'I want to have a look at her, don't try to move her'. He eventually decided that she had suffered a heart attack and there was nothing anyone could have done for her. She was a cow in first class condition and mothering a calf, such is the luck of the draw.

The local vet was a big man, and because he was bigger than my Father—and I thought he was big—to me he was very big and a little overpowering. He was a man of great deliberation, slow of speech and to me great in knowledge as well as stature! The first question he asked when called to an animal was 'Well, what is the matter with it?'

'I don't know', was the expected answer—even if you did!

Of a rule only two horses were shod—the ones that had to be used on the road to haul feedstuffs and pull the trap to town. Occasionally an un-shod horse would get a split in the foot where the 'frog'—the centre or sole—joins the hoof proper where sand or gravel would penetrate and cause the horse to become lame. The offending material was prised out with great care taken to remove it all, otherwise it could be a waste of time and possibly cause more serious trouble at a later date. The split was then sealed with clean material soaked in turpentine. An old shoe was then nailed on cold to protect the repair and, if possible, the horse was given a little time off.

Colic, a severe pain in the digestive system, sometimes affected the horses. This was not very dangerous, but appeared frightening if you had no previous experience of it. Generally it was relieved by a couple of measures of 'Black Drink', ingredients unknown, supplied either by 'Osmonds' or 'Hewthornes', two old established companies. Some swore by the one and some the other and I'm willing to bet that each contained exactly the same constituents.

Feet, hooves or clease (the cloven hooves of sheep and cattle) required attention more than any other part of the anatomy. Cows get what is commonly known as 'foul', sheep footrot, dogs split pads, and like people no animal can be content if the feet are sore. The remedy for 'foul' was poulticing and complete cleanliness followed by being kept perfectly dry. This sounds simple, but was quite difficult, cows being what they are. If an animal that is affected gained its freedom it would make its way immediately to soft ground and muddy places, almost as if it wished to be contrary, though in reality was looking for soft ground as it hurts less than hard. After the poulticing was deemed to have done its work the affected limb was given a liberal covering of Stockholm tar and hopefully cured.

Foot rot in sheep is the bane of the shepherd. A good sheep that develops it is a totally different animal in a matter of days. An infection finds its way into the foot, possibly through a slight fault in the hoof, and destroys the bond between the horn of the hoof and the softer inside of the foot. The detached horn is pared away, right to the living part of the foot, and a caustic agent brushed on to kill the infection. Regular treatment is necessary to control footrot.

Occasionally during the winter months one of the cattle would, for one reason or another, suffer from constipation which, if allowed to continue for long, then resulted in a complete stoppage of the digestive system with fatal results if not dealt with in time. The age old remedy was the 'Red' drench (again supplied by 'Osmonds' or 'Hewthornes'), which jokingly was said would move an elephant!

One of the most destructive of pests are maggots. To most people they suggest fishing, but not to a farmer. From late May to September sheep have to be seen daily and any sign of itching or discomfort has to be investigated. Flies lay eggs on a sheep which hatch into maggots. These burrow into the wool and cause the sheep to rub itself against trees or fences, or whatever proves available, even biting themselves to expose bare flesh. Sores develop, the maggots feast and burrow into the animal, more flies are attracted and the problem quickly spirals out of control if not dealt with. Through just a little oversight a good ewe or lamb can be more or less ruined, and at worst die if not caught early enough. As a sheep infected with maggots tends to go away from the flock and hide, a strict count has to be made each day so as to be sure that this has not happened. The treatment for this parasite then was

The winter of 1936. By some freak of weather the temperature near ground level was freezing, yet rain fell which turned to ice as soon as it 'landed'. On branches of trees, telegraph wires and wireless aerials it formed about an inch of ice, the weight causing some wires to break, and even branches to snap off. Sheep netting fences became solid walls of ice. Hay ricks had to be broken open with axes, and straw had to be strewn over the farmyard to freeze into the ice to give the stock some footing when they went for water

MacDougals, a carbolic acid based remedy bought in the form of a slab. A piece was peeled off and dissolved in water and the affected area soaked with it. Unfortunately it gave no protection against future attacks so something to repel the flies was needed, and here again was a use for the Stockholm tar. Occasionally a coat was made from sacks to cover the area.

Some animals were quite healthy, but just unlucky. Bow Horn was a first class Hereford cow. Her horns grew into the shape of a bow and turned up for a short distance from the tips, and did she know it. She used them to gain her position of 'Top' cow and kept it that way. She was a first class house cow as her milk was of good quantity and quality and either boosted the amount of butter for the house or provided a surplus for sale. (Often the house cow was not a true Hereford or in our case often not a Hereford at all—Darkey, my old favourite, was a Welsh Black, whilst Spotty was Ayrshire or cross-bred Ayrshire, but very gentle and docile for that particular breed.) Bow Horn's first calf was a nice Hereford, but oh boy was she hard to milk and she had a lot of milk for the breed. Whether the milk was richer than her calf could take I don't know, but the only thing that we could do to prevent scouring—diarrhoea—was to feed it about a pint of water after every suckling. Needless to say it didn't thrive and the same occurred with her next calf. It was decided to let her have a third and then to sell her with a calf at foot. She calved quite happily and we entered the pair for the next sale, but on the relevant morning we found a teat blocked, so we withdrew her. She developed mastitis quite badly, leading to the loss of one quarter of her udder and thus her value as a house cow, and once again her calf grew poorly. We decided we would eventually sell her as a barren cow. But before this could happen she became stuck in a bog on the Rhos where she died. It was not possible to reach her with a horse or knacker's lorry so we had to bury her where she lay. It does seem that some animals are born unlucky, but this was the most extreme case that I have ever had to deal with.

Dinner time on the farm was an occasion for good solid meat that would 'stick to your ribs' and last until tea time—snacks and light lunches were no use to someone who had to put in four hours of manual labour. Then it was off to feed the cattle again and very young calves to be suckled once more so as to give them a good start in life. The afternoon was then 'free' for any urgent or seasonal jobs until the cattle needed attending to again.

If the ground was frozen it was an opportunity to get rid of some of the accumulated manure. Hedging often took priority on such days as an insurance against having to stop doing more important work later in the year, such as harvesting, so as to return animals to where you planned to keep them. A certain amount of pride was also attached to hedges and gates, gappy hedges and dragging gates quickly established the occupier's position on the farmers' ladder.

Talking of hedges, during the winter there were hedging classes. It was deemed a waste to fell good oak trees to make stakes to use in the hedges so a system called 'Crop and Pleach ' had been adopted. A few living pieces were cut or 'cropped' at the height of the finished hedge, and at regular intervals in between living wood was cut with an angled cut until it was thin enough to be bent along the line of the hedge—'pleached', using the cropped sticks to hold the 'pleacher' in position. Experience plus tuition plus practice, a good eye and a sharp bilhook can work wonders and an overgrown hedge can be fashioned into a thing of art and beauty.

One of my father's favourite jobs was draining the fields. In this he had a great advantage, for he could use a divining rod, enabling him to detect old silted up drains and so save the endless heavy work that otherwise would be necessary to find them. In addition, where new drainage is being undertaken the dowser can find where the water is rising from underground and the course which it takes before it reaches the surface, so that the spring can be nipped in the bud in a manner of speaking. Laying drains in those days required plenty of muscle of the human variety and coupled with that, the application and will to do it. It took approximately 2,000 terra cotta pipes each one foot in length to drain an acre of land at a spacing of seven yards. Each trench would be about 70 yards long and up to two feet deep, depending upon the constitution and formation of the subsoil.

In farming at least one is moving about and the job has a certain amount of daily variety, but over all I found it very routine with nothing to occupy my mind. I fell into the habit of doing one thing and thinking of something else totally unrelated that was more interesting and more to my liking. This wasn't always advisable. The David Brown tractor which we once had did not run too well during cold weather when it was left to 'idle' for any length of time, and my thoughts turned to how to improve it. At one end of the range of farm buildings was a 'loose' cattle shed which was away from the normal feeding alleyway, or 'bing' as it is called, and their feed had to be carried across to them. At the other end of this range, facing the house, was the tractor garage. I went and cut a K(y)erf of hay, put it up on my shoulder on the pikel (pitchfork) to take for the bullocks in the loose box whilst my mind worked on my problem. I returned to the real world with a bump when I opened the garage door with the hay on my shoulder. I did an about turn as quickly as possible, but to no avail—I had been spotted.

'Have you fed the tractor this morning?'

'How are the bullocks off for T.V.O.?'

It took years to live that one down. Yet, I was thankful I was able to split my mind in this way. Such jobs as cleaning out the cowhouses and calf pens, or digging trenches for drainage were done and never was a spade 'seen' full.

As cowman it was my duty to attend to all calvings regardless. For example, I was a member of the Boy's Club, a social club which met on Tuesday and Thursday nights in a room above the shop and Post

Success in the hedging class of the Young Farmer's Club, of which by this
time I was an Associate Member, which you automatically became on
reaching the age of 25

Office at Abbey-cwm-hir, both of which were run by whoever was the tenant of The Happy Union pub, and this particular night Ellen would decide whether I went to the club or not, as she was due to calve. The calf, albeit a small one, duly arrived in good time, and I got it on its feet and feeding, Dad then saying he would go and keep an eye on it so that I could go to the meeting.

I arrived back from the club about half past ten to find Dad up waiting for me. 'Ellen has had another calf, surely you could see that the first was too small for a single?'

'Sorry Dad'.

'You'll know next time won't you?'

'Yes Dad'. That was Dad, once and once only.

As for corn, I remember the Green Piece, a field which we had opened up and unblocked the drains, and then ploughed, harrowed and planted with oats. In late summer it produced a lovely ripe stand, with a head on it like cream on new milk, rippling in the light wind. What a memory—and only a memory, for the wind came and the rain with it, down went all eight acres, leaving just a wisp standing here and there, a horrible sight. Unfortunately it happened all too often on the poorer land. The deliverer, or reaping machine, was useless, and instead the mowing machine had to be used to cut a swathe through the better part, which then had to be raked off the way so that the horses did not tread on it, then another swathe cut against the direction to which it was leaning. At the end of the run, the man on the mower jumped off and helped to clear that swathe, then it was back to the start to cut another. On one occasion he was helping to clear one swathe, having left the horses grazing on the hedgebank down the field, when an aeroplane came over flying low. The horses were frightened and started to run, taking the machine with them of course. Luckily they went at a tangent to the cut swathe and the waggoner was able to catch them, but not before the lines had been cut by the blade, though the machine itself survived travelling at least twice its normal speed. All that could not be cut with the mowing machine had to be cut with the scythe.

If a wet afternoon stopped all hay making but the weather cleared around five o'clock, then we had a prearranged system for organising a football match. We would drape a white cloth over a thorn bush in view of the neighbours across the valley and they would do likewise for others to see, and everyone who was available would assemble on a riverside field that one farmer gave us on a permanent loan for this purpose. We had held a collection amongst us so that we could buy a decent football.

Everyone was welcome—sons and daughters, brothers and sisters. There was no sex discrimination, and no favouritism. Two captains, girls or boys and chosen by common consent, picked their sides and we played for the sheer fun of it. Should there be a late comer they were added to whichever was proving to be the weaker team. When it became too dark to play on, we formed a sort of circle and we sang, and I mean WE SANG. We sang with our voices, we sang with our hearts and we put our souls into our singing to the exclusion of all else. 'Cwm Rhondda', 'Abide with Me', 'Cock Robin', 'Y Bwthyn Ar y Bryn' were some of the favourites, but we included whatever took our fancy, yet always finished off with 'Goodnight Ladies', singing it with all the feeling and bathos that we were capable of. The memory of that singing and the people who sang will live as long as I do; it was a cohesive collection of people, a group of people with bonds of friendship, grown and lasting, never to be broken by time or disagreement.

When I started as cowman, we relied heavily on horses. Fanny was our Welsh Cob, a chestnut with a white face and four white socks, pretty as a picture and as wily as they come. She was a good trotter and won both the Novice Trot and the Walk, Trot and Gallop at the local races. Plant a few pegs in a field and Fanny immediately slipped into trotting mode and wouldn't rest till she had completed a mile. When she was older we sold her to a riding stables to be used to give riding lessons to children.

It was often better to buy a foal from a neighbour where you knew the sire and dam—and the farmer to boot—than by going to a market or fair. Like people, horses have their ways, their temperaments and strength, but above all they have a high mental ability and a great sense of loyalty, and by buying a foal this way there was a pre-knowledge of its temperament. To breed one's own necessitated losing the work of the dam at quite a busy time of the year and that meant keeping an extra horse or pony, an uneconomic proposition, at least to us.

Horse Fairs took place in the late autumn and here the horse trader surfaced. These people usually had horses that were good looking and to all intents and purposes sound in 'wind and limb' and guaranteed G.W.A.G.—a Good Worker in All the Gears, or harness. Great care and quite extensive knowledge of horse and horse flesh was required by the buyer as some of these traders were adept in disguising faults or failings of the animals they offered for sale. Many a bargain proved quite the reverse.

Quite a common instance was that of slightly older animals that had been over driven and their breathing affected, but with treatment this condition could be hidden for a day or so. This treatment was as grotesque as the complaint, and how it caused the condition to be hidden I have no idea. On the day previous to that of the sale the horse was drenched, or force fed if you wish, with a mixture of lead shot and pig's lard or fat; perhaps the excess weight in the stomach prevented the roaring breathing which is an indication of Broken Wind. A farmer, not knowing, bought the animal and in a couple of days discovered it to be broken winded—the term used to describe this condition. As the animal was unsuitable for his needs he had no option but to sell it at the next opportune sale. Being an honest man he could not give a warranty as to the 'soundness' of the animal and had to sell it for whatever price was offered. At this point entered horse dealer number two, someone in the know, who usually offered a ridiculously low price for the animal, at the same time 'letting the cat out of the bag' regarding the horse and its fitness so ensuring that there would be no other bidder. To cut his losses the farmer sold unknowingly to one of the original vendors, a 'trick' that was then repeated as many times as could be, often at markets over a wide area, with potentially quite substantial profits.

Unfortunately there was no way of guaranteeing the elimination of a suspect animal short of slaughter. But do not get the wrong idea, most traders were straightforward honest people, and like everybody else tried to get as good a price as possible. 'Caveat emptor' held sway and if you paid over the odds that was your problem.

On one occasion of which I have personal knowledge, a horse having this condition was bought at the Newbridge-on-Wye Horse Fair in October whereupon it was discovered that the animal had been in circulation for some time. It was decided to put an end to this particular scheme and as the farmer involved had relatives in Cambridgeshire, the animal was secretly shipped there. The 'Gang' visited every horse fair within miles but of course failed to recover their money spinner. Finally they approached the farmer who had bought it and offered him a decent price for it as if it had been a sound and genuine animal, but were told that it had gone 'where you will never find it'.

The carthorse trade gradually ended upon the arrival of the tractor. The advent of this machine produced much discussion as to the merits of the tractor versus those of the horse. Some of the comments were quite ridiculous, with the youngest farmers making excessive claims on behalf of machine, countered by over the top suggestions from the older farmers on behalf of their four footed companions. One great advantage of the tractor was the ability to keep two beef animals in place of each working horse which would more than pay the tractor's running expenses. Another was that the amount of work that a man could do was at least trebled, making it possible for an operation to be completed when conditions were right as opposed to having to wait for suitable conditions to return at a later date.

The change was slow, with most farmers initially conceding that tractors were alright in Herefordshire, but that did not mean that they were any use in Radnorshire. Then a farming family from Herefordshire moved into the district bringing with them two tractors which they put to good use on a farm which local perception had it could never be made successful. As they persevered and seemed to thrive, local farmers still played it cautiously. 'Wait and See', or 'The proof is in the Pudding', or 'Time will Tell'—all delivered with a look of supreme wisdom that was supposed to quell all disagreement by the younger hopefuls. Gradually these Prophets of Doom were discredited and a couple of farmers upset the *status quo* by buying tractors, leading to the younger farmers putting on the pressure with an either/or approach—either we have a tractor or you drive the horses yourself—which eventually won the day.

Final resistance was broken down by the ploughing quotas that followed the declaration of war. These could not be met without the use of the tractor. At first the sale of horses would nearly pay for the tractor, but as tractors became ever more widely used, the customer for the carthorse became almost non-existent. Great ingenuity was shown in converting horse-drawn vehicles and machinery for use with the tractor until such times as money became available to buy tractor-drawn machinery.

The older farmers did take time to adjust. In one case a farmer was unable to start his new fangled machine which was at the centre of a sceptical enquiring crowd. His use of descriptive expletive was much to the approval and delectation of all around—apart from that of the vicar who had at first not been noticed. In the ensuing embarrassed silence, the reverend tried to be helpful, and said to the farmer, 'Possibly, John, if you tried giving it a nice pat as you would do to your horse and tell the tractor what a good tractor it has been it may even start for you'. To the amazement and consternation of the farmer, the tractor did indeed then start.

Unfortunately there were quite a few accidents on account of lack of knowledge of these machines—a few of them even fatal. The farmer, being an independent species bought a tractor, listened to what advice the salesman could offer, and then jumped on the seat and proceeded to put himself in more danger than he had ever been in before. Two brothers of mature years, tired of cutting chaff for the horses by hand and threshing with the flail on the barn floor decided, after much debate and deliberation no doubt, to have an oil engine to do these tedious tasks. The equipment was duly installed and they were given strict instructions not to start it for a week to allow the concrete on which it was standing to harden properly. No doubt it was a long week, but at last the day arrived to try their new toy. They went to the barn, no doubt in a state of nervous apprehension and turned the starting handle. Much to their surprise away it went. Then came the problem. How did they stop it?

Bill says to Bert, 'You started 'er Bert, You stop 'er!' So Bert, spotting a balk of timber which happened to be lying about, fetched it and attempted to put it in between the spokes of the flywheel in an attempt to stop the engine. Luckily the engine was going too fast to permit the wood to penetrate otherwise it could have been fatal. Success came an hour later when a neighbour was brought and turned off the petrol.

One result of this change to mechanical power was that fewer and fewer hands were needed. A ploughman could now sit on a seat and plough three or four times as much in a day, instead of walking 11 miles and man-handling the plough at each turn on the headland. However, one thing was for sure, the ploughman driving the horses had nice warm feet, but pity the poor tractor driver with near frostbite, and in the summer the hot sun up above and a red hot snarling beast underneath him.

We made our change shortly after the commencement of the Second World War, when we are able to purchase a tractor by selling two of the horses, a hard decision to take. It seemed almost like being traitors to them when they were so much a part of us as a unit, and no doubt it was hard for them to settle anywhere else. We could not help thinking about it, actually Dad went off somewhere when they were loaded to be taken away.

Our tractor was a David Brown, model V.A.K. 1, in Stark Staring Red, as it was described by a neighbour who had a Standard Fordson that we promptly referred to as being of a Bilious Green. She started on petrol and turned over to tractor vaporising oil (T.V.O.) when the manifold and engine reached working temperature. Sadly it ran on steel wheels, but rubber was getting in short supply and somebody had to be first—it happened to be us.

The old horse plough was useless and a brand new one had to be acquired—on the promise to plough a hundred acres a year in total. I dreamt that I would never have to follow a horse plough for 11 miles a day ever again; little did I know that part of my wartime

Our model of tractor—David Brown V.A.K. 1

work was to be on another farm doing just that. So much for dreams.

All that had to be altered on the harrows and cultivator or scuffles was the chain for pulling them, but adaptations for any vehicle with shafts and for the mower with its single pole to which the horses were yoked were a different matter. Many and varied were the adaptations ranging from the audacious to the ridiculous and dangerous, but they all had one thing in common, they were of the Heath Robinson variety.

Our next real buy was a side rake, a machine that would turn the swathes over at a much faster rate than we had been able to do in the old traditional way with the hand rake, one of the bottlenecks in the hay harvesting operation. The main bottleneck now shifted to the hauling, where the quantity that could be taken on the gambo was far below the capability of the tractor. A two wheeled trailer that matched the tractor became a 'must', and the local scrapyards were scoured to find a suitable front lorry axle on which to build one. Great minds think alike and all and sundry were doing likewise, but by a spot of luck we found an axle at one yard, a pair of wheels that would fit minus tyres and tubes at another, and, having a good friend in the motor trade, obtained a pair of worn out tubes with more patches than a tramp's trousers and tyres beyond use on the road. Those tubes were black market and were the most expensive articles of all—we joked that it wasn't the tubes that were expensive, but the patches.

The old gambo with the broken shaft provided nuts, bolts and irons to make a trailer that looked like an oversized gambo on under sized wheels, with a hitch made by the local blacksmith bolted on to its pole to couple it up to the tractor.

Building and repairing this machinery was the aspect of farming I most enjoyed. I loved mechanical things and always wanted to try and understand how mechanical movement or forces worked. The inside of a watch was far more interesting than the time on its face, or the windup mechanism of Mickey Mouse more so than seeing it run across the floor. Farm machinery held more for me than the finest cow or calf—I would far rather get my hands greasy pulling a machine to pieces, than lubricating my hands on the teats of a cow.

I bought myself a breast drill with a few twist drills to use in it, a hacksaw and a soldering iron for one and sixpence, postage included, from the Singer Sewing Machine Company who were selling off what in effect were worn out tools. Anyone going to Swansea was given 5 shillings to buy flint wheels for making ciga-rette lighters of different sizes, and with a stick of tin solder I was in business.

This was in the latter half of the Thirties, as the economy gradu-ally recovered. The most visible sign of this in the countryside was the increase in motor traffic, vehicles becoming owned by, gener-ally, schoolmasters, vicars, one or two of the larger farmers and certain businesses.

My own first mode of wheeled transport was the bicycle I was given at the age of 12. This old bike was rusty, its chain overly stretched, brake blocks worn down to the metal, and the seat springs very tired—but it was ridable. It also brought a constant chorus of 'Gi's a ride', and I soon learnt to use this to advantage, seeking favours in return. That bike provided 15 shillings worth of pure enjoyment—we all rode it, we all fell off it and it was a disaster if it was out of action for any reason.

Having worked for two years on the farm I was told that I was to have a new bike and was overjoyed. A Raleigh duly arrived. I remember seeing it for the first time when one of my sisters was playing 'For we proclaim Wales must be Free' on our piano, a tune that still conjures up the picture of a new Raleigh bicycle. That bike lasted me 15 years, in which time I rode it to death.

For some time my brother and I had been saving hard to buy a motorcycle, managing to put a little by from our weekly allowances. But it was only when I started to repair things for people and act as local barber at 6 pence a time, that cash started to 'roll in', relatively of course. All the savings went into a small box in the top drawer in our bedroom, until came the day when we had a whole £5 and 10 shillings. We had heard of a bike going for that figure and had it brought for us to see. I think we had bought it in our minds before we even saw it—a BSA 250c.c with one silencer missing and which slipped out of bottom, but it had two wheels, a petrol tank, an engine and gear box and that was good enough. We bartered away and got the price down to 5 guineas.

Returning to the house to collect the money to pay, we bumped into Dad. 'So you've bought it. How much?' We tell him. 'Have you got enough money to pay for it?'

'Yes and five bob [shillings] to spare' .

'That's alright then. I don't believe in borrowing to buy anything, If you haven't got the money to pay for it you wait until you have,' and off he goes into the house. (Dad only believed in borrowing if, as with the mortgage for the farm, it was the means for making money. In his eyes you just did not borrow to buy inessentials.)

We heave a sigh of relief, but then out Dad comes and hands a cheque to the seller. I could not believe my eyes and ears. 'Now', he says, 'you will have enough money to put it right, and if you can't you will have learned a lot more than if you bought a new one, and I'm sure you can't make it a lot worse so don't be afraid of it'. How true his words were.

We used all the petrol in the tank riding to the bottom of the lane and back, about a quarter of a mile, as we couldn't risk taking it on the road until we could licence and insure it. We also needed one new silencer, a new bottom gear, a kick start ratchet cog and return spring. In the stable was an old back number of *The Motor Cycle*, goodness knows how old, but it contained adverts for spares. Pride & Clarke of 158–160 Stockwell Road, London, advertised themselves as having everything on earth that was required for motorcycles. They could have spares for all the motorcycles on the moon as far as we were concerned, so long as they had spares for a 1930 250c.c. BSA.

The same model BSA that we had

We wrote out our list and asked them to be sent C.O.D.—in those days you could pay the postman cash for the amount of the invoice plus the postage. We then spent several anxious days watching and waiting for the postman, and then—The Parcel. The silencer was different to the one on the bike, but as no-one could see the two at the same time, what did it matter. Armed with a new set of spanners, zero hour approached. I shall never forget my first sight of the marvels of a gear box—lovely, shiny, smelly and oily! A mystery to be explored. Careful now, remember that the way it comes apart is the way it goes together in reverse; watch for springs and loose bits. It was all laid out in order, all the same way up, until I came to a cog that had some corners rubbed off, and, joy of joys, it was the same size and shape as the new cog with its perfect corners.

After much work it was reckoned to be usable and safe to go on the road and was licensed and insured. Both my brother and I had ridden an old Douglas twin cylinder with a belt drive and only two gears about the farm, but now we could sample our 'New' bike. With its chain drive it was not susceptible to weather conditions, but like all internal combustion engines it required a constant supply of petrol and oil, and financial constrictions limited its use somewhat.

It was not a good machine for night work as the lighting was provided by Calcium Carbide. A 'generator' let a controlled amount of water drip on to carbide of calcium which produced an inflammable gas that was conveyed by rubber tubing to a headlight and to a small red rear light that also illuminated the number plate.

This motorcycle was eventually replaced during the war by a Cotton 350c.c. with a J.A.P. engine, made by J.A. Prestwich and Co.—another step up in the travel stakes. It had twin up-swept exhausts, a four speed foot change gear box, pressure lubrication and mag-dynamo ignition and battery charging—the real Mc-Coy. But not until we found out what was the matter with it, for again we could afford to buy a 'pup'.

A more temperamental machine was never made. Tune it as best you could and it would run smoothly for a few miles, only to have to limp home, hoping your mates would not see you in this degrading state, wishing they would have been jealous of a properly functioning machine.

Much agonising and head scratching eventually spawned the decision to do a complete 'strip down', keeping going until the fault was found. We discovered that a bushed roller on the exhaust rocker had worn a 'flat' on it, and this caused the unreliability, depending whether it was on the flat or on an unworn part when it was adjusted.

We wrote to our tried and trusted Pride & Clarke to be told that the model was too recent for them to have a stock of spares and to contact J.A. Prestwich direct. They replied that there was a war on (as if we in Wales were ignorant of the fact) and as steel was a controlled substance (all we needed was a roller about five-eigths of an inch diameter by a quarter of an inch long) the part couldn't be supplied. Even the fact that the bike was wanted for use by a dispatch rider in the Home Guard failed to soften their hearts. I contacted all the local motorcycle dealers to no effect, and once walked nearly ten miles to find that the motor cycle at the end of the goose chase was a two stroke!

I would have to make it myself. I found a 'cone' from a bicycle ball bearing race that was only fractionally bigger, not that that would make much difference for it was the size of the hole through it that counted. For once fortune smiled, for the existing hole was too small. I drilled it bigger and fitted the 'bush' from the original roller, ground it to length and 'Bob's your flipping Uncle', as we used to say. The greatest pleasure for me was to show the person who thought that he had sold us a pup, that he was wrong.

The story is told of a certain man of the cloth who was desirous of owning and using one of these new motorcycles and made contact with the local garage owner to procure one for him. The machine was duly delivered to the clergyman's home. A ten mile, quiet circuit was agreed as the 'test' route and the customer, sat astride the machine, was given a complete run down on the procedure as to the use of throttle, clutch and gears. Being a man of above average intelligence he soon 'caught on' and set off on his circuit. In due course rider and motorcycle arrived but, to the garage owner's slight consternation, did not stop but continued on a further circuit with a shouted remark as it passed. Unable to pick out the words of the message, the garage owner waited on. Lo and behold the Reverend appeared once again and passed on as before, leaving the waiting vendor in such a state mentally and vocally that was not at all complimentary to preachers and parsons in general, and in language not usual when the company included these personages. Then, approaching for the third time, the noise of the motorcycle suddenly stopped—it had run out of petrol. The silence was palpable until the motorcyclist said, 'You didn't tell me how to stop it!', upon which they both laughed heartily and, needless to say, the motorcycle found a new owner.

Our BSA was well used, in part because it had a pillion seat. To call the pillion seat that would in fact be highly complimentary, for it was a small, hard cushion bolted on the rear mudguard and which was just a little softer and flatter than the mudguard itself, but then it was a seat and it was on a motorcycle and that made all the difference as far as the local girls were concerned. As my brother was quite a 'ladies' man, also having my share of that gift, he used the motorcycle to that end, whilst I was content to pull it to pieces and put it together again. In fact it was more fun when there was something the matter with it, and absolutely compensated for my lack of feminine companionship.

The BSA, and later on the Cotton, took my brother and I to town—Llandrindod—on many a Saturday evening, but this, too cost money. As mentioned, to supplement my father's allowance of 2 shillings and 6 pence a month, I earned money through a variety of means. As my mechanical ability improved I also manufactured cigarette lighters when such things were scarce.

Utility lighters were a government order during the war to replace the shortage of matches which needed timber and explosive materials, both of which were in short supply. Often these lighters were of very poor quality and the flint wheels became smooth and useless. If you used poor quality 'Pool' petrol to try and save money, then beware keeping it in a warm place for too long—notably in your pocket whilst at the cinema. The evaporating fumes stank and soon informed all in the vicinity what you had on you. After about four fills with 'Pool', the lighter had to be rinsed in petrol to get rid of the additives which by then had formed a camphorus, sticky, smelly substance, otherwise the lighter would simply refuse to light. These lighters sold at 6 shillings and 6 pence, and thus made for a good market for home made lighters at 5 shillings a time.

First I needed a piece of copper tube, size immaterial as each lighter was as individual as the case. My favourite was a piece of pipe about the same diameter as an old penny, for these could then be soldered on to each end of a three-quarters inch length of pipe to make the body of the lighter. My best effort, and which I still have even after offers very much above its value, is made from the case of one pocket watch with the back of another watch of a similar design. Its other components comprised the water filler screw from an obsolete carbide lamp, the lever from a shot or powder flask, a wick holder or burner—part of a valve core of a bicycle inner tube, a piece of so called sugar string as a wick, one flint wheel ex-Swansea, two small tubes and springs (one for pressure on the flint against the flint wheel and one to keep the wick cover in place in much the same way as the spring of a penknife keeps the blade closed), and cotton wool, whilst the cover and extinguisher is a cut down .22 shell or cartridge.

Over half our monthly allowance could be spent on a Saturday night out in town—4d. on half a pint of beer and a similar amount on a packet of Woodbines, followed by 6d. for a front row seat in the Kino (in Middleton Street, where the furniture people are now). The talkies had been showing for a short time, but my first visits to the pictures were in the days of the silent films, and at times you had to be quite a fast reader to keep up with the captions that came up on the bottom of the screen whilst coping with what looked like heavy and continuous rain falling down the screen.

One and Tuppence of our half crown gone by half past ten, then it was down to the Rock Park to the dance where Thelma Hammonds and her band dished up the most modern music, which could be heard far enough away for you to be 'In the Mood' by the time you got there. Here we could be lucky, for sometimes the doorkeeper got a bit fed up and had gone away, but more often than not we had to hang on until about 11 and then, looking as innocent as we were able, slipped in. They knew and we knew that they knew, but we would not have gone in if we had to pay, so nobody really lost out. At 12 o'clock it was 'God Save the King' and on your way, with four fags smoked, one for the way home and five left for the next week.

One day in the local shop the proprietor, nicknamed 'Long Bill' on account of his being over average height and having been a policeman in his younger days, mentioned that he had a car, a Standard 'Little Nine', which he had bought a while back, for sale for £50.

I mentioned it to Dad, but he was a bit doubtful as Dads always are, and as I was used to such doubt, it was no real obstacle. The next morning I took a can of petrol and filled the tank. He had kept the battery charged, but it still wouldn't start, so we cleaned up the plugs and carburettor, and pushed it out onto the road. Keeping our fingers crossed that Brooks (the Local Bobby) was not around, we let it roll downhill, and gave it a try. It started and the deal was clinched.

It was a bit noisy but it was a car. It had lost patches of paint and had an engine like a bag of nails—the prospect of many hours of pleasure to come. It looked like a matchbox on wheels with a sunshine roof as a finishing touch.

I concocted a compressor out of our old BSA motorcycle engine and a smoothing chamber from a five gallon drum with a relief valve, bought a spray gun and some air line and got it all fixed and working. After a small amount of welding and filling on the body-work I proceeded to spray the whole car, making a respectable job of it—to the extent that two years later the car was sold for two and a half times as much as it cost in the first place. Then it was the turn of the mechanics. The engine was rather weak, and to use an old saying 'would not pull the skin off a rice pudding'. As with the Queen of Hearts in *Alice in Wonderland,* I decided 'Off with her head', and had an almighty shock. Bits of piston rings had broken their way up into the combustion chambers and were either riding on top of the pistons or had found their way out through the exhaust valves—at least there were not nearly as many pieces as there should have been judging by the amount of rings missing. The bores were scraped and cut about, and it was marvellous that it

71

would go at all. Norton's, the local garage, were able to track down new pistons and re-bore the engine.

As soon as the car was running again we sold the Cotton motor-cycle at a decent profit, which went part way towards paying for the car—of which my father and mother came to approve in place of the motorbikes.

During the war there was at first a 'basic fuel ration' which applied to all private vehicles, but as the war progressed this was replaced by the requirement to apply for a ration for the following month's estimated needs. Business trips, markets, phone—the nearest kiosk was three miles away, doctor—five miles, chemist—six miles, all incalculable and necessary. It often happened that an urgent journey arose out of the blue, that by definition had not been included in the application, yet to make it was an offence. If discovered it could lead to disastrous consequences such as the withdrawal of all supplies.

Early one October a stock tup, or ram, had become lame on his hind feet as a result of footrot and as such would not be able to carry out his duties, much to his chagrin and disgust as well as ours. The only remedy was to find a replacement. As it happened there was a sale of rams at a market not too far away, and at no small risk the decision was taken to go in the car and try and purchase one. Parking was limited to the extent that only one place was vacant— right in front of the Police Station. Timid is he who loses, Bold is he who wins, and so parked it there we did. No questions were asked, a ram was bought and everybody lived happily ever after!

My interest in mechanics also strayed into the house. Initially candles provided light inside whilst a paraffin lamp, often referred to as 'the Gordon', was used for outdoor work. Gradually the candles were replaced by paraffin table lamps, except to go to bed which was often accompanied with the instruction 'Mind not to drop any wax on the stairs', which were bare boards for years.

My brother and I discovered that if you spat saliva on to the top of the candle it would stay alight long enough for you to get into bed before it spluttered and went out, by which time you were settled down and all snug. But, as often is the case, there was a downside, for the candle was loath to light the next night and our little trick was soon forbidden. It did, however, set off a new train of thought. The lights in the bicycles and motorcycles had been fuelled by carbide of calcium, but battery lamps were coming into use and every now and then needed replacing as their power faded. Nevertheless, if two of them were connected in parallel they would still provide a useful light. We linked these in a circuit with a bulb in a redundant socket to a block of wood which we fixed to the bedhead in which was set a door key. When this was turned it formed a connection and caused a current to flow, so providing a light that could be switched off after getting in to bed. Heath Robinson maybe, but it worked.

Downstairs the Gordon was superseded by a pressurised oil lamp with a mantle which gave a very bright light, but it was not handy for carrying about from room to room, and dangerous to take in buildings where there was hay and straw due to the heat it generated. I literally burned my fingers on one of these pressurised lamps.

Due to the war these lamps were scarce and as I had an old model available I decided to update it.

Strangely enough, although the lamps were virtually unobtainable, spares were easy to get, so I bought what spares I considered necessary and fortunately the screws and nuts were similar sizes and threads. I initially made a mock up so that I could find out whether my idea would work or not, but I did not heat it properly before I attempted to light it. Hot paraffin streamed down the sides of the vaporiser, hot enough to make the paraffin burn like mad but not hot enough to cause it to vaporise in the tube and so provide the necessary back pressure. I turned off the fuel supply and carried the whole 'flaming lot' out of the house to burn itself out. The next attempt was successful and that lamp was in use until electric lights were installed.

An enterprising relation of my own age had bought and installed a small electric lighting plant at his home, but contracted T.B. and as there was no one beside him that could properly maintain and attend to it, it was offered to me. I was only too pleased to have it. I raided the local library for any sort of book that would furnish me with useful information, whilst my friend helped me dismantle the whole set up. The truth is that that was one job I would rather forget, for this was when the only cure for T.B. was open air treatment and hope; I felt as if I was taking the life of someone who was heading nowhere. I am pleased to say he fully recovered, but I always had that feeling of guilt as if I had made things worse for him.

Then came the job of installing it in our house. I loved wet days as I was 'let off' to work on it. The engine was a one and a half horse power J.A.P. with a 25 volt generator—actually a warming up gener-ator for aircraft engines—which charged a couple of high capacity army tank batteries. Used sparingly one charge would supply light for a week to all rooms in the house.

One of these batteries came to a bad end, though it could have been worse. A cigarette smoker at that time, I was hovering over the batteries on charge with the stoppers taken out of each cell as advised for that particular make of battery. I must have gone too close for the battery exploded and acid went everywhere—in my face, in my hair and on my clothes. I made a dive for the water butt, and I mean a Dive! I went into that barrel as far as I could, yet still have a fair chance of coming out alive. They say that a little knowl-edge is a dangerous thing, that is as may be but I know it is costly too, for all of my work clothes were spoiled, not to mention the need to buy a new battery. Fortunately the only marks that I received were yellow speckles on the whites of my eyes; I tremble to think of what would have happened had that water butt not been there. Quite a patch of the cement of the floor came away with the acid to be a permanent reminder of my carelessness.

CHAPTER IV
Marriage Rituals

A couple who got married between the ages of 15 and 50 were closely observed to watch for any portents of an addition to the family, such signs indicating the date of conception and therefore whether it conformed to the rules of the critical. In most cases a birth was welcome, but if there were already too many in the family it had to be tolerated, and at worst, if the parents were not wed, it was considered a disgrace.

Often a guessing match took place amongst the 'knowing ones', and if it was a little 'early' generated such remarks as 'I expected it', 'Always was a flighty piece', or maybe 'Never should have been married in white'. Strange how this type always crawled out from under their stones in times like this, and if the truth were told maybe were no better than the ones they were slandering, only doing it to persuade themselves that other people were worse than they were. At the other extreme, if a pregnancy did not happen immediately the remark was, 'Not for the want of trying I'll warrant!', or if it did 'At last he's proved himself a man'.

Such people were at least in the minority, most people being only too pleased to see a family started as that meant continuity and a family not dying out. In one case a couple had 21 children—twice, or so it was put round by a local wit. After this couple had had 21 children, some of them 'farmed out', one died and they then had another—sufficient information for the local wit to weave his story.

This was an extreme, but families of eight, ten and twelve were not uncommon, and all often had to cope in a small cottage with only two bedrooms and two downstairs rooms. Yet, most of these children grew up healthy and strong, apart from the weakly at birth, and above all there was no asthma. True, a deformed baby or one unhealthy at birth often failed to live for long. A case of the survival of the fittest it is true, but there were no aids or accommodation in those days to keep such babies alive, and though I risk contradiction, it often meant that a lifetime of shall we call it a 'Half life' was avoided.

In the early days young people met by going to church or chapel under the watchful eye of their parents who tried to manipulate the acquaintances of their offspring, oblivious to the fact that the youngsters were as clever as their parents in avoiding the desired contacts. As most people rarely met anyone from outside their own parish, except for the occasional hired worker, there was often surreptitious control of the community by the elders of the church and the deacons of the non-conformist chapels.

As time went on and people got a little better off, farmers acquired ponies and traps and that extended the distance travelled and isolated areas became less so. With the improvement of the roads the bicycle came into use. Generally speaking this was the real start of the end, as it made it possible for the son to slip away after chapel or church to the neighbouring village and there make contact with the opposite sex. However, to all intents and purposes this was enemy territory, no-one was going to let one of their girls be stolen by the next village or parish and this led to many a difficult and, in some cases, dangerous situation.

A favourite ploy was to allow the visiting suitor to think that all was proceeding smoothly, allowing him to see the girl home, then somewhere on the way back he was ambushed, the ambushers having provided themselves with a goodly number of 'clods' of turf liberally soaked with water. The first thing that the visitor knew was a volley of wet and sticky clods, his only hope being to make a run for it, in truth to run the gauntlet with a lot of well armed locals to contend with. It needed a brave man, or one very much in love, to face that a second time. But some did and eventually neighbouring villages more or less amalgamated. When the motorcycle and the car came along, barriers created by distance were further broken down.

No longer was the local patriarch able to hold sway; his judgment was no longer law, and some of the local privileges that pertained to his position no longer applied—actually a great social divide was swept away. It also brought about a great change in

76

Llandewi Church

thinking. When there had just been the parish, the thinking was communal—the neighbour and his family was considered along with your own—but with a greater exchange of people, occupations and ideals the community spirit was eclipsed, and 'a look after yourself and let others do the same' feeling became the norm.

Sadly this attitude became evident in the marriage stakes. Instead of marrying the neighbour's son or daughter with similar likes and dislikes and with whom you had more or less grown up together, the desire became to marry someone who would improve the financial or social standing, irrespective of understanding and compatibility. Girls did not stay at home any more, instead they took jobs in shops, offices and hotels where there was the chance of meeting a suitable partner. Yet, this change was quite understandable taking into account the restrictions to which people had been subjected under the old system.

A side effect was that the urban girl was not likely to accept the conditions and isolation of the rural boy, and this sometimes left the farmer's sons without a wife or housekeeper, and no chance of a son to take the farm on after his time.

As far as weddings were concerned, much effort went into the reception which, on a farm always took place in the barn. Volunteers would spruce the place up, flowers would be placed at strategic points by the ladies, with most attention going to the top

Howey Baptist Chapel decorated for a wedding. This is where I and Vera were married, as well as each of our parents. The organ was used till the Fifties when it fell into disrepair, and was only restored to working order in the summer of 1995

table where 'auntie's' cake received pride of place. It was considered good manners to say that this cake was the finest yet, thus also making sure that aunty would be flattered into making another for the next family wedding, and that if possible to transcend this one.

The barn was filled with a variety of cutlery, plates, cups and saucers belonging to sundry owners, and in assorted sizes and colours—most people only had enough to sit themselves and a couple of guests down to dinner or tea. As subsequent identification could be a problem, each lender wrapped a little coloured wool or cotton around the handles, the result original and quite pretty. The variety continued into the glasses—the only attempt at evenness of approach was in the quantity of contents! As the day wore on, out from a dark corner would come the 'home made', notably elderberry, rhubarb, and an old-time favourite for the dry wine fanciers—whitty berry, or rowan or mountain ash. All potent and imbibed with caution, they were guaranteed to put a sparkle in the eyes of the girls and hair on the chests of the men.

As out with the corks went caution and inhibitions—the bride-groom got some verbal stick, a lot of gratuitous advice, and the bride hints as to the way to get the best from her new husband which, as the wine flowed, increased in strength and innuendo.

While the home made was passing around the male members graduated to the back of the barn where the small barrel of beer had so far lain undisturbed, and by some magical process they all now had large glasses as befitted the latest beverage. The visits to see the latest calf got more frequent, accompanied by a surreptitious little flicker of the eyelid.

In the interest of economy there was no honeymoon, the money being better spent on getting started and as the married couple were not 'going away' the partying went on as long as people could, before going home to do the necessary chores on the farm. Everyone who so desired was presented with a wine bottle filled with any beer left in the cask, but only after the singing stage was reached, a normal thing and reached quite early in Wales. Then Father Time had his way—there were cows to be milked, calves to be fed and preparations for night, and the company gradually dispersed leaving the parents and the young couple.

Of course there has to be a joker in every pack, and the joker had been busy while the ceremony was taking place. A bell may have been wired under the bed, or a tin of Andrews Liver Salts put in the 'Gosunder'. One trick that was really past a joke was to cut horse-hair—mane or tail—into short lengths and strew them in the bed. This was diabolical as it made the bed impossible to sleep in and ruined the bedclothes for ever.

When honeymoons away began to be taken, this brought new opportunities for the pranksters. A small stone introduced under the backband of the trap harness of the pony in the trap prepared to take the couple to meet the train would cause quite a commotion before they set off, until the cause was diagnosed and removed. Then when the car took the place of the trap the joke had to be up-dated; a wad of wet blotting paper was introduced in the top of the high tension coil which, as the engine warmed and the paper dried out, formed an insulator. Too bad if the driver did not 'know his onions' and had to call for assistance.

Another harmless joke was to wire a couple of kippers to the exhaust. This happened to yours truly, but I had an extremely good and intelligent friend—Carlo the sheepdog. Carlo fancied a bit of kipper for dinner, and what Carlo fancied Carlo had if it was at all possible.

It often happens that the groom has a special or close friend that whispers in his ear details of the impending doom, and so is able to take evasive action.

One of the best evasive actions I have seen was taken by a member of my family, a sagacious sort of chap who thought up a scheme to thwart the machinations of the 'enemy'. Half a mile or so from the reception hall there was a railway crossing with gates, the crossing being able to be reached from either side from where the reception was to be held. The crossing keeper was a good friend of the groom, a friendship no doubt enhanced somewhat with the price of a couple of beers as he was asked to close the gates for the 4 o'clock a little early. Meanwhile a staged leak indicated that the couple would leave by way of the upper road, and so the ambush car was placed in a strategic position on this road.

At five minutes to four precisely, the couple got into their car, and the friends took off to theirs. Off go the bride and groom along the lower road, their friends, deciding they had been duped, promptly did an about turn to get on the same road. When the friends caught up with the groom's car, they thought they had them after all—only to find that the car had been abandoned, the couple having walked across the line to another car that was waiting for them on the other road and, now waving goodbye to their erstwhile tormentors, went peacefully on their way.

CHAPTER V
War

My brother was the bearer of the news that war had been declared. He had gone into town, partly to obtain a replacement accumulator for our wireless, the charge in the existing accumulator having failed that morning, and we had lived in complete ignorance of the fact for some hours, not that it made any difference to us or to the war.

The wireless, a Pye 5 Valve, was about as much weight as I could lift and was quite a powerful set for the day. It required an aerial, and we stretched a wire between the two nearest trees, giving a line well in excess of the legal length of 50 feet (the length that was supposedly 'in tune' with the wavelength of the Home service). It was while erecting this aerial that I climbed too high up one of these trees, its top bending over to the horizontal leaving me suspended below some 30 feet above the ground and hanging on with my two hands. Gradually moving my hands back along the tree, the weight balance shifted and the tree returned to a more upright position. The aerial ended up attached lower down the trees than was my first intention.

With this arrangement we even managed to hear some American programmes during the night, albeit with variable sound, including a boxing match involving Max Baer or Rocky Marciano, I forget which. The accumulator would sometimes fail or become discharged when something of importance was being broadcast, one of these unfortunate failures occurring when Winston Churchill was making his 'Blood, Tears, Toil and Sweat' broadcasts. Panic stations would erupt, the six volt battery would be taken off the motorcycle, one cell of the three connected to the accumulator terminals with spring clothes pegs and Churchill was saved without him knowing anything was amiss! Sadly this was the beginning of the end of our wireless, for my father subsequently connected up across the full six volts with the result that he had a few decibels extra for a minute, but this was followed by a long and permanent silence.

It may seem strange that one of the emotions on first hearing of the outbreak of war was the hope that it would improve the economics of farming, but initial excitement was followed by concerns as to what it would mean for each one of us in the family, and for the family as a whole.

My brother, then aged 20, had registered for National Service when the system started some three years before the war. With the advent of war his work on the farm, coupled with the fact that our father had the 'Rheumatics', a word that covered all types of arthritis in those days, earned him the status of having a 'reserved occupation', which was subject to periodic review. If his status changed he would be called up for the Royal Navy for which he had expressed his preference and had been accepted. My eldest sister was registered as a milk maid and poultry woman and so, too, was exempt, but my other sister was called up into the Civil Nursing Reserve.

We listened to the news of the invasion of Czechoslovakia and Poland. For once officialdom moved with surprising speed, issuing instructions as to how many acres we should plough and what we should plant in those acres with a mental agility hitherto unknown—though as was usual with total disregard of people, conditions and type of farm.

Our acreage under the plough was increased to virtually double what it was before. Fixed acreages were to be planted with potatoes, wheat and barley. Any wheat and barley grown in excess of the stated area was commandeered leaving only oats to feed the bacon pigs. If planted in the wrong soil or conditions, wheat and potatoes can yield less than the amount of seed planted, but appeals were largely useless. A sense of frustration prevailed, for seed had to be bought at an inflated price due to a shortage, and often the quality was low, at the same time knowing that the cost would be greater than the saleable product when the crop was harvested, entailing a season's hard work only to lose money. Artificial manures were rationed by shortages and distribution difficulties which made for low yield of corn and poor grazing for animals. Yet there was no excuse for shortfall in the required output and in some cases farms where this occurred were taken over by the War Agricultural Committee. Vegetables, apart from potatoes, was the one area where you could grow and eat as much as you were able.

Instructions were issued by the War Ag. as to what acreage was to be put under potatoes, payment being made on the acreage planted and not the crop harvested. (It would have been difficult to set a realistic target for what our farm, for example, could produce on land not normally used for growing potatoes.) The area was inspected periodically and measured meticulously, and an estimate given as to the weight of potatoes expected to be harvested. A poor crop did not cover the cost of cultivation and seed and subsequent weeding and earthing up, whereas a good crop created storage problems as it was not until February or later in our area that the official buyer was authorised to take your crop. In the meantime a monthly return of all stocks held was required by the powers that be.

It was important when planting the area of land for potatoes, that you planted an acreage as close to that of your quota as possible. If you planted less you would be financially penalised, and if you planted surplus, you were still only paid for the acreage given in the quota. Headlands at the end of the rows were excluded from the area deemed to be under cultivation, and this often caused complications as many fields were odd shapes. In addition, inspectors often just measured from the centre of each boundary fence, however that related to the shape of the overall field.

However, when the War Agricultural Committee ploughed, harrowed or drilled a particular field the payment was levied on the O.S. acreage of the complete field, regardless of shape, as measured to the centre of a hedge or to a wire fence. The field in which we chose to grow our quota one year was roughly circular, making the headlands at the sides of the field very short indeed—much to the consternation of the inspector—and compared to the O.S. figure the difference could be as much as half an acre. With a pencil and paper he calculated how much land should be at the sides and ends of the potato rows had it been a square patch, which produced a lower figure than we had calculated, and firmly stated that 'his' area would be the one allowed when calculating the acreage in fulfilment of the quota. I argued that his figure was low in any event, so he produced his official tape and instructed me to stand at one point on the boundary whilst he traversed the field in the direction of the potato rows paying out his tape as far as it would reach, then waited for me to go to him and stand on his mark while he went forward again, and repeated the process until the field was measured both ways. Now it must be admitted that, having control of one end of the tape, a little guile was used to counter this situation which was considered grossly unfair and was used solely to return the goal posts to their proper place. Quota fulfilled! Cheating? Not in my book. The field cost more to cultivate on account of its awkward shape. In addition we had laid pipe drains in that field on which there was a subsidy, and if the calculations of the inspector been followed we should have been deprived of some of that income too.

Certain restrictions also had to be imposed to ensure that agricultural produce was distributed fairly. The first ration books went into operation in the second week of January 1940, less than six months after the declaration of war. For the most part the food allowance was calculated on the basis of a single person per week. Over the years, the amounts were varied depending upon available supplies. Some items were transferred to a points system, which enabled you to choose when to take these within a time limited period. In May 1941 cheese was included in rationing, with those who were registered as manual workers having a higher allocation than others. In 1942 the allocation of eggs was 29 per person for the year, though with special allocations for children and expectant mothers and those with young children. Generally the system worked well, but a black market thrived on the side. The most active was that of dressed poultry, particularly at Christmas time when it included turkeys and geese. Slaughter of any livestock on the farm was prohibited, and all livestock had to be taken to the local sale yard and graded. The amount of edible meat (excluding offal) was estimated and the producer paid for that amount, that also being the part of the animal that was officially rationed, but at a ridiculously low value. The price given for poultry were such that it did not pay to rear and sell them, which acted to depress the supply. The only exception to this rule was the farm's bacon pig. Yet to obtain a permit to kill the pig and acquire the necessary salt, all the bacon coupons allocated to all the inhabitants of the household—even if there were separate 'units' of the family living in part of the house— had to be surrendered. This proved counter-productive as some

SUPPLEMENTARY CLOTHING COUPON SHEET   SC5G

UF 162636

Name
(BLOCK LETTERS)

Address
(BLOCK LETTERS)

(town)   (county)

Nat. Reg'n (Identity Card) No.   /   /

IMPORTANT.—These coupons may not be used unless the holder's name, full postal address, and National Registration (Identity Card) Number have been plainly written above IN INK.

CLOTHING COUPON   CLOTHING COUPON

CLOTHING COUPON   CLOTHING COUPON   CLOTHING COUPON   CLOTHING COUPON

CLOTHING COUPON   CLOTHING COUPON   CLOTHING COUPON   CLOTHING COUPON

Supplementary Clothing Coupon. Standard Coupons were issued to everyone, Supplementary ones to those who needed work clothes—such as farmers and mechanics

people preferred to retain their coupons, and so deprived the total food supplies of pigs which more or less maintained themselves on roots, nuts, acorns and such like for the greater part of their lives.

At one time anyone with over 21 laying hens were required to take all of their eggs to the Egg Packing Station, even those which had been damaged, and buy back their ration. So as to be exempted from this requirement many farmers and smallholders reduced (or so they said) their number of hens. Even so, the producer had to be registered with the Food Office and was issued with a rubber stamp displaying their name and the letter B in the centre of a circle with which to mark every egg. The eggs so stamped could be sold to registered retailers without them having to go through the grading process, but the shopkeeper could only sell these eggs to customers on production of their 'Egg' coupons.

In this way the eggs from the small producer entered the rationing system. Strangely enough cracked, shell-less and double yolked eggs did not have to be declared. This is where Humpty Dumpty came into his own, and boy he worked hard!

As the graded eggs were stamped with a letter A it implied that those stamped with a letter B were somewhat suspect, and this led to opposition to the use of the letter. Many producers decided to stop using it, just stamping the eggs with their name. As this practice became commonplace the Food Office thought it best to leave well alone.

When a producer sold his eggs to the approved retailer he was paid the 'controlled' sale price for them and when he bought his ration of his own eggs back again he was supposed to pay the 'controlled' purchase price which was more than he had sold them for a few moments earlier. What a strain on one's honesty!

One loop-hole was eggs for hatching. Many a 'sitting' of eggs ended up in the pan or the cake and on many an official plate too, accidentally of course.

One animal outside the rationing process was the rabbit. Good old bunny, but after endless meals of roast rabbit, fried rabbit, casseroled rabbit, and stewed rabbit we became a bit fed up with him. Surplus rabbits were caught and sold to the local trader who delivered them to Birmingham and even London at the rate of tons per week. Other relief came in the shape of the occasional hare, pheasant or fish—together with corned beef. An entry to a local limerick competition went like this, (taking into account that the fresh meat ration was 8d. per person per week):

> Meat at eight pennorth a pill
> Is enough to make anyone ill
> But for relief
> Take a little Corned Beef
> Says Dr. Edith Summerskil.

Dr. Edith Summerskil was the Minister of Food.

The days of war were dark days and so were the nights, only doubly so, with the whole country blanketed with blackout curtains. Motorcycles were fitted with 'masks' similar to those considered suitable for cars. The trouble was that our motorbike had carbide lighting and when you put a mask over it the blackout was 99 per cent effective—it was equivalent to trying to drive by the light of a candle in a jam jar.

Luckily for us, but not so for him, a friend of ours who was more enthusiastic than competent managed to put his similar machine beyond all possibility of repair and we were donated with the resulting wreck. The luck was that his mag-dynamo was repairable as was the headlight, albeit with the use of insulating tape and soldering iron. Now we really did need a mask or we would certainly be in trouble, so mother was instructed to find us a full size fruit can or buy one if she couldn't (fruit and all) and let us have the tin A.S.A.P. Coupled with a piece of galvanised iron for the base, the glass in the lamp was soon replaced—and we had tinned fruit for tea in the bargain.

With petrol rationing, the push bike was used as often as possible, but its light batteries were often on the wane. One day I became involved in a conversation with the local bobby as the evening light grew ever dimmer. I hoped he would finish the conversation and wander off, but in the end, I turned the bike away from him, switched on my light in preparation for my homeward journey and prepared to mount. As I did so he moved casually in front of me and remarked in a gentle sort of way that 'The light on a vehicle should be in view from in front of the said vehicle, and in your case it is, provided that you get close enough'. This was a friendly way of saying, 'You had better get a new battery before next Sunday night'.

In due course I was able to buy and fit a friction driven dynamo on my bicycle. This dynamo had one peculiarity, the further you went the more the light increased in brilliance until after a few miles at a good speed the light was as bright as or even brighter than those of many cars when they were fitted with the regulation masks. This resulted in me being stopped by a warden when returning from visiting my aging grandmother on account of my 'emitting an excessive amount of light'. Once again a tin was resorted to, of smaller diameter this time, and the light was duly dimmed, only for lightning to strike a second time. Doing the same journey a short time later, out into the middle of the road steps the same gentleman, right hand aloft in the recognised stop position. The actual words that followed are lost in the mists of time, but the gist of it was that my light was too dim and I was 'putting other people at risk' and 'had a total disregard for the law'. After a lengthy explanation as to the modifications that I had made and a thorough examination on his part he agreed that I was within the law and complying with the lighting regulations, rather grudgingly I fancy.

It was not long before the Local Defence Force, the 'brigands and bandits' of Lord Haw Haw, was formed. We were issued with armbands with L.D.V. stencilled on them and drilled with broom handles—with a little imagination you could get by. As most of us farm people had 12 or 16 bore shotguns, which loaded with number two shot could be very effective and dangerous, these gradually replaced many of the broom handles. One or two were even issued with cartridges loaded with a single ball, but were not used as the ball was too big for a gun that was fully choked (had a reduced bore) and there was a danger of the gun barrel bursting, presenting a greater danger to the user than the target. One .22 rifle turned up a couple of times, but it proved difficult to use in the drill sequence so disappeared again. We were a motley crowd, but with murderous intent as far as the enemy was concerned.

The next piece of armament that arrived was a Lewis machine gun, not the heavy water-cooled type favoured by the army but a lighter air-cooled model, at one time used in aircraft, that had a magazine holding 97 rounds if filled completely. The instructor set it up on its tripod on two card tables and sat the proposed machine gun crew around it. The gun was stripped down and re-assembled and an empty magazine placed in position. Holding the trigger and taking the cocking handle backwards and forwards the magazine was seen to revolve the distance required to feed one round into the firing chamber.

The instructor then announced the next part of his programme. 'When the gun has been fully charged and not fired, it has to be disarmed, and this I will now demonstrate'.

A few rounds were loaded into the magazine and placed in position, and the magazine was turned until a round engaged in the loading pawl. 'I will now demonstrate how to remove the magazine, but as the round is locked in the loading mechanism the only way to get it free is to go through the actual loading sequence without the magazine in place.'

One of the lads was sitting directly in the line of fire of the gun, and I said to him to come and stand to the rear, only to get quite a mouthful from the instructor as to his abilities and competence as opposed to my complete ignorance.

'Now,' he says, 'we will proceed with the unloading that we have had interrupted. The cocking handle is gently pushed forward until there is a click which tells you that the extractors have caught in the grooves in the round, then the cocking handle is brought back where the round is freed and ejected, like so!'

There was an almighty bang, a bullet ripped through the one card table and pierced the panelling and lodged in the stone wall, whilst the cocking handle returned with so much force that it caused serious damage to the instructor's hand. The room itself was full of smoke from the exploded cordite. To the best of my knowledge that bullet is still lodged in the wall (the hole itself has been filled), and I sometimes think that had I not moved that lad that the damage could have been much more serious than a damaged hand.

Whether it was a case of having the right name I could not say, but despite the episode in the hall I was put in charge of it and was assigned the other two members of the crew.

After a crash course, it was off to the firing range. In the words of the instructor, 'The Lewis gun is spring fired, gas operated, trigger controlled'. The pull on the return spring for firing the gun was weighted with a spring balance to 14lbs. which gave the necessary force to activate the loading mechanism, send the round into the firing chamber and fire it. When the bullet neared the end of the barrel it passed over a hole that allowed the gas pressure to escape and force a piston back to the position where it would collect another round and so the cycle was repeated. When the trigger was released then the forward movement was arrested and firing stopped. At least, that's what they told you. This time it kept going.

'Take your finger off the trigger you *** idiot'.

'I haven't got my finger on the trigger, sergeant'.

The force delivered to the spring was balanced by an arrangement of four holes of different sizes: if the force to the piston was insufficient because the hole was too small then the gun would fail to collect another round and so stop firing, the remedy being to test the next largest—before going into action of course! My theory is that enough gas power was delivered to collect a round but not enough to engage with the trigger and continued until the magazine was empty. By this time, a matter of a minute and 97 rounds later we were left with a gun frizzling hot, me a nervous wreck, an exceedingly irate sergeant and the whole of our ammunition allowance gone for a 'Burton'.

Whether it was a freak occurrence or a machine fault we were not told, but that particular gun was replaced and thereafter magazines had to be loaded with three rounds and then a gap, so that a maximum of only three rounds could be fired before it had to be manually re-set. I trust we would have been given complete magazines if we'd ever been unlucky enough to have to use the gun in action.

Sergeants from a local army unit were made available as instructors both for drill and weapon instruction. As every fresh instructor brought a different weapon with him, we soon knew a respectable amount about a variety of military weaponry.

Despite such knowledge, you couldn't hide the fact that a lot of the 'regulars' thought we were enthusiastic amateurs and bunglers to boot, although we were the means of a break in their routine.

There was one serious problem, however. Everyone was welcome to join, and join they did—the lame, the halt and the blind, and none could say them nay. Luckily many didn't stay long, except for a few who became the bane of the bunch. But there was a group that were more dangerous than these, and they were the ones who didn't know the business end of a gun. They had to be made number two on the Bren or the Lewis machine guns to keep them out of mischief, and to make sure that they were no danger to us or themselves.

One night a huge bundle of uniforms arrived, dumped in through the door of the hall. 'Sign here please. Thank you.'

Bits of uniform were soon spread from the door to the far end of the room, all mixed up. Trousers long and trousers short, blouses fat and blouses thin—it appeared that we had all the misfits from somewhere. Strangely enough most eventually found a blouse and trousers that would do or could be made to, and all that was left was one solitary pair of trousers. Our current drill instructor—an old soldier from the Great War with a vocabulary to match—was in the habit of lubricating his vocal chords in the local over the road prior to putting us through our paces, and had followed this hallowed procedure on this night. The scene that followed his regal entrance is indescribable, and the verbals unprintable. He picked up the lone pair of trousers and shook them like a dog shaking a rat, then caught it by the bottom of a leg and beat it on the floor disturbing the dust that had lain undisturbed for at least five years.

'Can't go anywhere for one **** moment, and all I get is ****, **** trousers that would fit a **** elephant.' He punctuated each **** by taking two steps forward and giving another slash at the floor until the room was full of flying dust. Finally, short of breath and epithets and four letter words an uneasy peace was restored as the dust settled on everything and everybody.

This evening, in addition to our drill instructor, we had our usual instructor who had thoroughly enjoyed this exhibition. As he had some connection with the uniform distribution he told the drill instructor that he would take his measurements and 'have a word', as he put it.

Rifles were so far conspicuous by their absence, but that ended one night when there was a scare. We were called out about midnight to find a dozen rifles had arrived to supplement our armoury of shotguns. We thought someone must have raided the army's Pandora's box, but when we examined them it looked more likely to have been the British Museum, for the guns were wrapped in oiled paper, the bolts, breech and barrel full of vaseline that was semi-solid with age. There were no pull throughs, not that they would have been of any use in any event, but we needed to remove the thick gunge by some means—if someone had tried to fire those rifles as they were he would have blown himself to kingdom come. A well grown but thin hazel stick was found that with a little trimming would slide through the barrel, and this was used to prise out much of the vaseline, before the balance could be removed with boiling water.

Then someone noticed that we had just ten rounds of ammunition between the 12 rifles. A phone call was made and a further 100 rounds materialised from somewhere. At about 2a.m. blankets were issued, along with orders—I was to stand guard. I took a turn around the outside every ten minutes, returning to the warm and to the wheezing and snoring of about 20 men. Four played cards all night. At 7a.m. we were told to stand down—the emergency was over.

I headed back home on the old BSA (though our pet name for her was BitSA—Bits of this 'un and bits of that 'un) loaded with one 12 bore shotgun and one dubiously clean Ross rifle. A quick change of clothes, grabbing of breakfast and it was out to feed the animals—the usual procedure whether the 'stop out all night' was enforced, or of your own volition.

Shortly after this last episode a batch of Lease Lend rifles arrived—Remingtons and Springfields with a very limited amount of .300 ammunition. The rifles were issued with only a few slings for carrying them over the shoulder. My brother had been promoted to the position of despatch rider on account of us having the motorbike, and needed one of these slings if he was going to be able to carry a rifle whilst riding, but wasn't issued with one. It so happened that there was a strip of 'webbing' about the place that by chance

91

was the right width and had an adjustable buckle. All that was needed was a length of brown button thread to stitch the one end to the sling mounting bracket. I blancoed the home made sling and thought it real posh.

It so happened that my brother was unable to attend the next parade for some reason or other, so I decided to adopt the rifle, slung it over my shoulder and made my way there on the motorcycle.

'Parade! Fall In', and I duly did so.

'Number one, second rank, left turn. Take two paces, March. Halt. Right Turn. Four paces forward March'. One minute of dead silence. 'Your name?'

'Private Lewis, sergeant'.

'Is that your rifle, Private Lewis?'

'No, sergeant, it's my brother's'.

'Oh, so it's your brother's?'

'Yes sergeant'.

'Then what are you doing with it?'

'He couldn't come tonight so I brought it to drill with me'.

'Does he know that you have his rifle?'

'Yes sergeant'.

'He does, does he? Then he is guilty of breaking the rules, and in war time that is a serious offence'.

'Sorry sergeant'.

'I was under the impression, Private Lewis', the 'Lewis' heavily accentuated, 'that rifles belong to His Majesty's Government, but you tell me that this rifle belongs to your brother and that he has had the audacity to lend it when it is not even his to lend. And by the way I note that an unlawful piece of equipment has been attached to this rifle by yourself or your brother and that is another breach of the King's Regulations. And I order you to remove the offending attachment immediately or face the consequences'.

I duly snipped off the stitches with my pocket knife, rolled the offending article up and put it in my pocket for 'future reference'. Then I was marched back to my place.

Strangely enough, this incident was a turning point in the relations with the Regular Army people. This particular sergeant never showed up again, and we gained the impression that a report of the incident had reached a place of authority.

We were also given grenade practice. On one such occasion there were too many of us and we were split into two groups; I was in the non-grenade party—luckily as it transpired. One of a batch of faulty grenades exploded prematurely, killing one of our lads and forcing the instructor to be invalided out of the army, and he was one of the nice ones.

One of our duties was night guard on a railway bridge. This bridge crossed the river in a long slant and as the one side of the river was high ground and the other low, the bridge was quite a length so as to maintain a gentle slope of track. Due to its length it was considered a vulnerable target for bombers, particularly on a moonlit night with visibility enhanced by reflections off the water.

The guardhouse was a railway workman's hut about a hundred yards from one end of the bridge and held a small amount of coal, thanks to the help of a stoker or two, for heating purposes. In the event of the bridge being damaged, we were supplied with a number of detonators to place at least half a mile from the damage. These contained an explosive charge that detonated when train wheels passed over them, loud enough for the train driver to hear and stop as soon as possible (we had no phone). These had to be placed so as to lie on the surface of the rail and were held in place by two flexible metal 'clips'. That was fine for our side of the river, for we could quickly run half a mile or so down the track that way. But what about if the bridge were blown up? We would then be faced with swimming the river on a freezing night whilst making sure that we kept the detonators dry, running half a mile or so, placing the detonators and then making the return journey to seek the warmth of the hut. The hope was that you could place them before any goods train arrived at the bridge. Luckily we were never called on to do this, there being only one occasion when we thought we might. One night a German plane circled low two or three times, but then went away and dropped his load to the north of us with little or no damage.

A neighbour, who also had a motorcycle, and myself 'did' our night from 10p.m. to 7a.m. every Thursday and our brothers every Friday. That way we had a motorcycle to get to and from the guard-house and our opposites had one between them should it be required.

One weekend, after I had done the usual Thursday night guard then my day's work on the farm, I went to the local dance and stayed until midnight, when all dances and social functions had to end. On Saturday morning there was a light frost and as it was dry the job was to plough the 'Bottom Meadow'. It was a beautiful day, with no wind and the sun shining.

Dad said 'I'll bring your dinner down to you so as to get as much done as possible, I'd like to see it all turned over today, if you can manage it'.

'If I don't turn over first', I thought. Was I tired! The sun was warm and so was the tractor—and the desire for sleep was overpowering. When my dinner arrived I had difficulty in eating it as I was so sleepy. Sheer willpower kept me awake, for I wanted no restrictions placed on my future attendance at the local dances. Finally the field was ploughed, and I was off to bed as soon as it was reasonable. At 10p.m. a motor arrives. Invasion threatened. Report to headquarters at the double with full kit and weaponry.

The night was frosty, and after reporting at headquarters I was transported ten miles in an open lorry to a central point in the 'Company' area, so we could move as quickly as possible to any point. By that time I was fully awake for the first time in 48 hours. We stood by until mid-afternoon, when the emergency was declared over—and very welcome too.

The time came when Winston Churchill renamed us the Home Guard and our unit became the Second Radnorshire Rifles. Subsequently a 'mobile unit' was formed, for which a local businessman had three lorries pressed into action along with his private car. Each section had its own lorry: Number One was the so-called Recce or Reconnaissance Section, Number Two the Stop Section and Number Three the Assault Section. The car, as you would suppose, became the 'headquarters' car, and in addition there were two Dispatch Riders on motorcycles. Broadly speaking the Reece Section had the duty to seek out and find, the Stop to give covering fire for the Assault to attack—at least in theory.

I was promoted to corporal in charge of the Stop Section. Apart from the Lewis gun we were also issued with a Sten and 70 rounds of ammunition. This gun we nicknamed the watering can on account of the fact that you pointed it in the general direction, pulled the trigger and sprayed everything in sight and range. (The Bren was the opposite of the Sten—it was deadly accurate. As was usual when we were introduced to a new weapon, the instructor stripped it down and then called for a volunteer to assemble it, the volunteer generally being—'You there'. This time it happened to be my brother who was quite good with mechanical things and willing

The Mobile Unit: No.7 Platoon, 2nd Battalion Radnorshire Rifles
The author is in the centre of the middle row,
and his brother is third from left in the back row

to have a go, and did, but was left with a couple of 'bits' spare. The instructor teased him in a good humoured way. 'Clever boy, got a couple of spares eh!')

Our squad was one of the best in the area and was often selected for duty when the reputation of the Home Guard was likely to be criticised. On one occasion we had to stand to attention for two hours in full battledress, including steel helmets, with our backs to the afternoon summer sun. But we didn't always live up to our reputation.

The fact that there were three of us by the name of Corporal Lewis was in itself a recipe for disaster. During one night manoeuvre a certain message resulted in myself and one of my namesakes throwing thunderflashes, representing hand grenades, at each other. Had it been in action it would have been a disaster of some magnitude. After that incident the two of us were known as Corporal Recce and Corporal Stop Sec.

The comparison with 'Dad's Army' was remarkable in its likeness to us both in action and personalities. The company commander, Major Barnard (in the centre of the front row in the photograph above) was as like to Mr. Mainwairing as any two peas, the platoon commander was Uncle Arthur's twin and the platoon sergeant, though not a butcher, had a considerable physical likeness to Jones, though there this likeness ended. Our first lieutenant and platoon sergeant, both veterans of the 1914-18 war, were past their sell-by date but cottoned on quickly and took us with them. As for variety we had a doctor, a blacksmith, a milkman, a quarryman, drivers, farmers, a postman and a shopkeeper.

Our company commander was of the opinion that we needed toughening up, and with that in view ordered a double length parade once a month. As most of us were engaged in activities of a strenuous physical nature, as opposed to the company commander's rather sedentary occupation, we found his decision odd.

One Sunday, as one of his 'double parades', we were dropped in full kit in a village more or less at the foot of Radnor Forest, where maps were handed out on which a route had been marked up and over a spur of the mountain in the general direction of another village. 'There will be a cup of tea when you get to the objective'.

Tea was rationed and our allowance turned out to have been drunk by the headquarters staff by the time we got there. Well, what could you expect, they'd had to sit for two boring hours waiting for us lucky blighters who had something interesting to do and look at! For a double parade we were normally paid a subsistence allowance of 7 shillings, a useful bit of pocket money for us, but here was the rub. If tea was provided this was forfeit, so we were faced by no tea and no money. Then came the final blow—we were to march back by road to where we had set off from.

Tempers ran high but we were persuaded by Uncle Arthur and Mr. Jones to march, provided that our company commander marched with us. Accidentally on purpose, our platoon took the front spot. The company commander took his place at the head of the column with his walking stick at the ready. 'By the left, Quick March'.

'Match my step', whispered Uncle Arthur, and off we set at Quick+ March, pushing Captain Mainwairing. After half a mile comes the order, 'Parade. Halt. Anyone who wants to fall out do so and the transport will pick them up'. No-one took up the offer; the sport was too good. 'By the Right, Quick March'.

The following mile was not quite at the double, but the company commander had his heels trodden on a sufficient number of times to remind him that the time for games was over. Suffice it to say that double parades seem to come to an end, whilst any parade exceeding four hours unerringly produced the regulation tea or cash.

One August Bank holiday was spent in camp. The Officer Cadet Training Unit stationed in Llandrindod Wells were given leave over this period and it was decided to use their mountain training camp over the weekend for training the Home Guard.

About 40 volunteers, truly so this time, piled on to the lorries on the Friday night to arrive at the camp to find that the canteen sold beer at a penny a pint less than the local. Our Jonesy war veteran, a rather good performer on the customer side of the bar, came into his own and full glasses constantly replaced empty ones. The bar closed at about 11 and we drifted off to our eight-man tents, where we slept feet toward the tent pole and head to the outside, the rifles and other weapons piled at our feet. Our tent contained the NCOs, including our beer consuming sergeant.

All was quiet until our sergeant believed he was back in the trenches, somehow managed to force his head out under the edge of the tent, thought that the Germans had got him and that the tent was coming down over our heads. Two of us grabbed a leg each, but this only confirmed him in his idea that the Germans had us surrounded. Those legs took some keeping hold of. Eventually we dragged him back into the tent and untangled his head from it, calmed him down, reminded him where he was and led him outside to let him come to terms with nature.

Being so tired I quickly went back to sleep only to awake later and realise that our sergeant was not with us. A search party was formed, and we found him at the bottom of a steep bank by the side of the river where there was a strip of sand; had he rolled a few yards further downstream he would have been in quite deep water with no sand to save him. He had no memory of either rolling or walking down that bank.

Before breakfast next morning we had a two-mile jog and how he did that run I have no idea. The weekend was spent criss-crossing the mountains, the Sunday in a fine drizzle. Somehow our old sergeant was still with us at the end of each day when some younger men had to be left behind.

On the occasion of the Home Guard sports day, our platoon won several of the competitions, and we were invited to the local for a little refreshment after our gallant efforts. The landlord filled the flowing bowl, as did our platoon commander and a few others who were now in the right humour to do so. Two old stagers, both sergeants, survived to turning out time, as they had oft before. Their routes home only gradually diverged, and so they were able to talk to each other over a slowly widening distance.

'You alright John?'

'Aye, you alright Bill?'

'Aye, aaalright'.

Two minutes later and further apart, 'You alright John?'

'That I be. Mighty dark though, can't see much. You okay Bill?'

'Aye, see you tomorrow', but by now getting too far apart to properly hear.

Five minutes later 'You alright John?' Received no answer.

'You alright Bill?', but too far apart to hear.

John became worried and thought he had better go and see if something was wrong. Bill, too, was worried and thought he'd better go and see if John was alright. Both arrived back at the local and both were pleased that the other was in fine shape. They reaffirmed their vows of friendship and off they set again.

'You alright—'. When or how they got home is not recorded, but one thing is certain, neither remembered it next day, which is just as well really.

Periodically we had proficiency tests set by the 'Brass', which were quite tough if you were an NCO. The booths used at elections were placed along both sides of a big room, into which we were marched and directed to the next empty booth. Our platoon sergeant was more practical than learned, and certain precautions had to be taken to preserve his rank; I was detailed to keep him close company in the examination room. We hung back so as to be in the second detail, so we could assess the procedure.

'Next detail, Fall In'. The sergeant and myself positioned ourselves together near the front, marched in and dropped in to two adjacent booths. By now we had discovered that there were a set number of questions and a fixed time in which to answer them. The divisions between the booths did not quite reach the table and we had worked out that I could pass him bits of paper with what I hoped were the answers. He was under strict instructions to pocket the bits of paper; jokingly we advised him to eat them.

I had to work fast to write both my own answer and his, and slide the paper under the partition for him—not always easy as we were being supervised. I spent a week worrying whether I had failed him

A.F.W 4026.

Certificate of Proficiency
HOME GUARD

No. 100/4026/3.
Date 4 Mar '44

...Training Establishment, Primary Training Centre or Recruit Training Centre, the holder must produce this Certificate at once for the officer commanding, together with Certificate A if gained in the Junior Training Corps or Army Cadet Force.

PART I. I hereby certify that (Rank) *Cpl* (Name and initials) *LEWIS G.F.*
of *B* ~~Battery~~ Company *2 Radnor* ~~Regiment~~ Battalion HOME GUARD has qualified in the Proficiency Badge tests as laid down in the pamphlet "Qualifications for, and Conditions governing the Award of the Home Guard Proficiency Badges and Certificates" for the following subjects :—

Subject		Date	Initials
1. General knowledge (all candidates)		2 Mar '44	
2. Rifle		2 Mar '44	
3. 36 M Grenade		2 Mar '44	
*4. (a) Other weapon ..	Sten	2 Mar '44	
(b) Signalling			
*5. (a) Battlecraft, ~~(b) Coast Artillery, (c) Heavy A.A. Bty.~~ ~~work, (d) "Z" A.A. Battery work, (e) Bomb Disposal,~~ ~~(f) Watermanship, (g) M.T.~~ ..		2 Mar '44	
*6. (a) Map Reading, ~~(b) Field works, (c) First Aid~~ ..		2 Mar '44	T.C.T.

Date *4 March* 1944   Signature *H.C. Farrer, Maj.*
* President or Member of the Board.

Date_____194__   Signature_____
* President or Member of the Board.

Date_____194__   Signature_____
* President or Member of the Board.

Date_____194__   Signature_____
* President or Member of the Board.

Date_____194__   Signature_____
* President or Member of the Board.

PART II. I certify that (Rank) *Cpl* (Name and initials) *G.F Lewis*
of *B* ~~Battery~~ Company *2 Radnor* ~~Regiment~~ Battalion HOME GUARD, having duly passed the Proficiency tests in the subjects detailed above in accordance with the pamphlet and is hereby authorized to wear the Proficiency Badge as laid down in Regulations for the Home Guard, Vol. I, 1942, para. 41d.
Date *4 March* 1944   Signature _____
Officer Commanding
Commanding 2 Radnorshire Batt. Home Guard.G.

The Certificate of Home Guard Proficiency awarded to me in March 1944,
perhaps surprisingly in light of some of the stories told here!

as well as myself as I had so little time to consider and write the answers. As luck had it we both passed. If the truth had come out we would have been reduced to the ranks for sure, but as it was I was for a short time the toast of the platoon.

In 1941 I was old enough to commence my National Service, my brother having being given a further six months' extension of leave, now being the main man on the farm. As expected my papers arrived telling me to present myself for a medical examination at Wyle Cop School, Shrewsbury on 20 August, along with a free rail pass to get me there. I hoped to join the RAF for which I had expressed preference on my enlistment form, seeing it as a way out of the lifestyle that I had been obliged to follow. My thoughts were a mixture of expectations coupled with doubt with a little guilt at the possibility of leaving my family.

On arrival I was sent down a corridor into a well-lit classroom. 'Strip', which I did apart from my Y fronts. 'STRIP', so away goes my modesty at a stroke. I was given a small glass and shown an apology for a cubicle. 'There is a bucket in the corner if you need it'.

There followed a series abrupt commands and barked information. 'Stand here'; 'Height five, five and a half'. 'Sit Here'. 'Here' was a set of cast iron scales that I should think they kept in a fridge. 'Stand here'. 'Bend over'. 'Cough'. I was prodded and poked here and there. 'Stand up'. 'Breath in'. 'Breathe out', again and again. Thump here, thump there.

'Dress up. Straight down the corridor and knock at the door straight ahead, and wait'.

I do, and eventually a voice says 'Enter'. Again I comply. A very smart RAF officer sat at a huge desk with what looked much like my school attendance register.

'Name?'

'George Francis Lewis'.

'Occupation?'

'Farmer'.

'Farmer? FARMER?'

'Yes sir.'

'Then why the heck put barman on here?'

'I didn't, sir'.

'If you didn't, who did?'

'Couldn't tell you, sir'.

He grabbed the papers and went off at a rate of knots—or whatever Air Force personnel do—his body language saying 'you better be right mate'. Two minutes later he was back and slammed the door with such force that the place shook. By now I had lost any self-confidence and assurance that I had had.

'Farmer?'

'Yes sir'.

'Age?'

'Twenty-one, sir'.

'Married?'

'No sir'.

'Religion?'

'Baptist'.

'Baptist?' said as if I was some sort of strange animal.

'Yes sir'.

Then ensued a lengthy examination as to my knowledge of engines, machinery, elementary electrics and wireless on which I was able to give a reasonable account of myself, but I had to admit to no academic achievements.

'I see here that you wish to be a pilot?'

'Yes sir'.

'Fighter or Bomber?'

'Either sir'.

'I'm afraid it will not be either.' I wondered why he had bothered to ask the question.

He filled in his register and gave me my forms back to deliver to their office. In the space for his decision was marked 'A.F. 21 RAF'. I still do not know to what position that code referred.

Back home I had to await the outcome, and when it did there was no Air Force for me. Instead I had to work half time at home and half on another farm where there were not enough people to carry out the requirements of the War Agricultural Executive Committee. I received the same pay as a private soldier—12 shillings a week. Agricultural wages were actually 26 shillings a week, a sum which my employer paid to the War Ag., who then retained 14 shillings before paying me.

Both farms were in fact under-staffed and the hours were beyond what any paid worker would normally contemplate, on top of which there was four hours parade with the Home Guard on Sunday, two hours on a Thursday night and the one night guard duty on the railway bridge.

During her work with the Civil Nursing Reserve, my middle sister came into contact with many soldiers who returned to the country in hospital ships, one of whom was Ken.

Ken had been taken prisoner at Dunkirk and served time in prisoner of war camps first in Germany and later in Poland where the treatment was much worse. In due course he was repatriated on an exchange basis, a privilege granted to those who were not likely to survive in their present circumstances. He was mentally scarred and was no longer really interested in living. When they had completed all that they could do for him in the medical sphere, my sister wrote home to ask if we could have him for a while to see if it were possible to help break the downward cycle into which he had fallen. It would have taken some one very callous to refuse and we certainly did not.

Ken duly arrived, a wreck of a man, but where there's life there's hope. It was very difficult at first to find anything that interested him. In time we discovered that he could play the piano very well, but a man cannot play a piano all day. Occasionally he would get out one of our old paint boxes from the time when we were children and he would paint flowers, particularly roses, that looked really life like, as well as portraits of us that were remarkable likenesses.

He was a man of quiet disposition, asked for little and appreciated all that was done for him. On one occasion I said, 'I wish I could do things like you can'.

His reply, so characteristic of him, was 'You can do very many things that I cannot, so we'll call it quits'.

Then one day my father said to him, even though it was a bit of a risk with him in the state that he was, 'Would you like to take the gun and see if you could find a rabbit and shoot it for tomorrow's dinner?'

An hour or so later Ken rolls up with a rabbit and with a brighter look in his eyes than we had ever seen before. From then on things got better. When it came to harvest time he drove the tractor, and though he was very amateurish and wasted a lot of time, it released a man for other jobs and also gave Ken the satisfaction of doing something useful.

It was our custom to go to chapel on a Sunday evening. It was a break from the routine of the week and there was always the slight hope that a local girl would smile kindly in our direction, though as most of the local girls were either in the Forces or munition factories we generally had to be content with the outing. By the time Ken was with us even most of the land army girls had gone home, to be replaced by POWs, many of them Poles who had fought with the Germans. They tended to keep themselves to themselves and that bothered no-one.

However, one Sunday evening, as it was coming dark, we happened to see one of these POWs on his way to the hostel where they were billeted. Ken said 'good evening' to him in Polish, only to be answered with a stream of words unintelligible to me, but clearly not to Ken. Rarely have I seen a man whom I'd always seen as placid and friendly, suddenly change so markedly. He backed the Pole into the hedge and frightened him to a whimpering state, then stood back and said something. The POW looked visibly relieved and went on up the road, albeit looking like a dog with his tail between his legs. I have no idea what was said, and never dared to ask. I had seen a wolf.

When he was as fully fit as he was ever likely to be he returned to his own home, but came regularly to see us. At the end of one of his visits, my father said to him, 'Ken, the old gun is not used any more, would you like it?' It had deteriorated over time and we had bought a replacement.

'Oh,yes', he says, and father brought it for him. I shall never forget that moment. Ken took the gun with both hands and the tears ran down his face. It took a few moments before he could say, 'Thank you. It means so much to me. That gun saved my life, it gave me the will to live'.

Some years later Ken married and had a home of his own, but he never forgot us as long as he lived.

Working the long hours on the two farms I was often too tired to even go as far as the local or to the local hop, or dance, but even if you did the available ladies were few and far between and you faced stiff competition from men in the Forces. With the arrival of the American soldiers the position was even worse, for they were more popular than the local lads—they had money, cars, cigarettes and drinks in abundance. It is a very unfortunate fact that these troops did not endear themselves in the locality, and with those old enough to remember, there is still a little niggle when American soldiers or personnel are mentioned. The perception is that they smoked our 'fags' which they professed not to like, drank our pubs dry, filled all the seats in the local cinemas and crowded or cleared our dance floors with their Boogie Woogie style of dancing, and never an apology for anything however rude or crude. All this was coupled with a 'You ain't seen nothing yet' attitude.

One incident sticks in my memory. One late afternoon I cycled into town in the hope of going to what was supposed to be a good 'picture'. I can't remember if I gained entrance to the Pivi—the Pavilion—but I can the vacant place at the end of the evening where my bike should have been. I had to walk home as the local bus had already left and I did not have enough money to take a taxi.

I borrowed my mother's bicycle to go to chapel the following day, it being Sunday, and thence to Crossgates where I happened to

In the years when our Country

was in mortal danger

GEORGE FRANCIS LEWIS

who served   25th June 1940 - 31st December 1944

gave generously of his time and

powers to make himself ready

for her defence by force of arms

and with his life if need be.

George R.I.

THE HOME GUARD

The letter of thanks received after I left the Home Guard

see my bike being transported on the back of a police car on its way to the police station. Next morning I rang the station and was told that the bicycle was being held pending enquiries after being recovered near the local American army camp in an undamaged condition, for which I was very thankful. As for apprehending the culprit, they knew and I knew that they knew that any enquiries were as futile as shooting at the moon, but to satisfy protocol my bike stayed at the police station for six weeks.

In due course the Home Guard was disbanded and we were told we could keep our battledress and greatcoat but, strange as it may seem, a pair of knitted gloves issued to me for use with the machine gun had to be returned to the local collection point or I would be charged for them.

Even with the ending of the war, rationing and deprivation continued, and problems were compounded by the winter of 1947. On Friday 24 January the Young Farmer's Club of which I was a member had put on a three act play in the Iron Room at Penybont, and quite a success it was too. We left with snow falling heavily, but managed to coax the Standard Little Nine home, though little did we expect that it would be the last time it would be on the road until mid-May.

When we got up the following morning the snow was still falling, the windows of the downstairs rooms were half covered with drifts of snow and the back door was completely blocked. On opening the front door, the snow fell in right to the bottom of the stairs. The road to the buildings where the cattle were was blocked, the gate had disappeared completely and we had to make a detour through the meadow to reach the buildings.

Feeding these animals was not a problem when we reached them but getting them to water was another matter, as was reaching the out-lying cattle at the bottom end of the farm. Wellies on their own were useless, and we wore cloth wound around our legs like puttees to keep the snow out and our feet dry. By dint of enticing the out-lying cattle with sheaves of oats we led them to the homestead and some kind of shelter with enough to eat, but again water was the problem. There was no lack of the stuff, but getting them to it was another matter—the wind was howling like the Banshees driving and blowing the snow horizontally, and the water lay under ten feet of snow. The air temperature was minus 17 degrees Fahrenheit. Most of the day was spent in digging a way to the water but the snow kept filling up the roadway that we had dug.

We were completely exhausted by the time that the snow abated, but even then the wind went on drifting the powder. Its surface looked unreal as about the top inch was blown about, appearing as a low-lying mist and obscuring the true surface. At last we cut a clear road through to the water, only to find that the cattle would not go into the 'canyon' that we had formed. The problem was solved by carrying fresh dung from the cowhouses and strewing it along the track to make it look as if cattle had already been along it.

Next day it was the turn of the sheep. Here we were lucky, for quite a few of them had bedded down where the snow had not covered them and the sheep dogs soon discovered what we were doing. I shall never forget for as long as I live the pleasure on the face of those dogs as they stood on the drifts of snow and looked down with their ears cocked and the tail doing nineteen to the dozen. When you arrived they didn't have to be told to 'find another', they just did it.

One rather curious and unexpected finding was that the sheep which had been buried were much better off than the ones that had not. The loose powdery snow came easily away from the wool, whilst that on those in the open froze and formed lumps which varied in size from marbles to golf balls or even bigger which combined to create a heavy load for these sheep to carry. When they walked or tried to shake their bodies in an attempt to rid themselves of this burden, they made a most unnatural rattle, and when going round at night during lambing time it was quite uncanny.

When a ewe had difficulty in lambing, which was far more frequent than in normal circumstances, the ewe had to be taken indoors, for it was uncomfortable for man and beast to handle a sheep at minus 10 degrees Fahrenheit or less. Never at any time during this period could the flock be left to itself—when lambing, a ewe lays herself flat on her side and with the extra exertion tends to expel more hot breath than usual; when lying on grass this is no problem, but on snow or ice it could be. As the long winter had already caused most of the ewes to be in a weakened state, a ewe would often reach a point where she could no longer hold her head up and would drown in a matter of minutes if no-one was around to help. In an hour she would have been frozen to the ice.

The total lamb crop was one third of normal, with no saleable older ewes. The only thing not frozen was the mortgage payment and that was due on 25 March, come rain, hail or sunshine—or snow.

Grass was never seen from that day in January until the first week in May. Snow on parts of Radnor Forest lay higher than the telegraph poles and was estimated at over 30 feet deep. People from a village several miles north of us on their way to get supplies had to guess where the road was because the fences and hedges had disappeared, and at a very sharp bend miscalculated and actually crossed a ravine. If the snow had given way they would have stood little chance of surviving.

Bread rationing was held in abeyance and bread was delivered by tractor and pony. Our home baking was a thing of the past for the simple reason that the roof of the baking oven was starting to collapse and loaves had a habit of being sprinkled with bricks and mortar. The rebuilding of the baking oven would have been a major undertaking even if it had been possible to find a builder with the necessary expertise, not to mention the cost which would subsidise the bread from a baker for years. Bakers had started delivering bread to the door at very little extra cost to baking at home, but during this period the nearest that the baker's van could get to us was at least three miles away. Bread was a necessity and the only way to reach it was by tractor and shovel. The old Standard Fordson was charged into the drifts of snow until it was forced to stop. Then it was reversed and the resultant packed snow was cleared, an operation that was repeated over and over again.

For the first mile the route lay across the direction of the wind which meant that the roadway had been filled with drifting snow up to hedge height. Once the lane curved round we found that the wind had swept parts of it clear and was largely passable with the tractor. It was one of the longest journeys that I have ever travelled, starting out at day-break and arriving home with a sack filled with bread after dark.

Weather reports gave hope of a thaw several times, but each failed to materialise until one morning, when looking up, a spot of water from an icicle a foot long hit me in my eye. What joy! It felt as if we had been let out of prison. Where snow drifts had reached into the branches of trees, rabbits had eaten the bark from the exposed wood, and when the snow disappeared a white line was left where the bark had been eaten. Much of the wood above this line subsequently died from a lack of sap. A sorry sight indeed.

With the thaw came a warm wind and with the wind rain, inches of it. Rivers flooded, ice nine inches to a foot thick piled up against bridges, and trees on the river bank had the bark stripped away at anything up to ten feet above the river bank. Hedges and fences were torn up bodily and left where chance decreed.

Damage to houses and buildings was severe and in some instances hay barns were lifted bodily and deposited some distance away as a mangled mess of wood and corrugated iron. A few of the more lucky ones were stripped of their corrugated roofs and left standing like skeletons silhouetted against the sky. Only through desperate emergency repair was our barn saved from destruction.

Six-inch long nails were driven through the 'Zinc'—the local name for galvanised corrugated iron—with large washers under their heads to keep the sheets from flying away, during which operation the ladder had to be tied to the uprights to prevent it and me from being blown away—and this was done in the dark in a torrential downpour. The water was coming off the roof straight at me and by the time it was finished I can truly say that there was not a dry rag on my body, even my wellington boots were full to overflowing.

Strange as it may seem, when the snow finally disappeared the grass was found to have been growing under it, a very welcome start for the sheep and lambs.

The first corn was sown on 17 May, a date that sticks fast in my mind. The 'Big' field was the first to be ploughed and worked up on the 16th ready for drilling the following day, having sufficiently dried out before any of the others was dry enough. I had made prior arrangements to go to Knighton's hiring and pleasure fair due to take place on the 17th, one of the special annual events as far as we were concerned. I told my father about this arrangement the night before and he said, 'Alright with me, BUT that field has got to be drilled before you go'.

The cows were eating their morning fodder at six o'clock the next morning, the suckling of the calves and the milking was completed by eight, the necessary watering, cleaning out and feeding all done by ten. Soon the seed in its sacks and the corn drill was standing at attention in the big field. I got started before dinner, which I downed in ten minutes at most—my deadline was to catch the bus from three miles away, at five in the afternoon. Just after four I completed the last strip, jumped off the drill and let the driver carry on, ran home, shaved, washed, changed clothes, and was on my bike. I left the bicycle in a yard that was safe and jumped on the bus with my mate with seconds to spare.

What we did at the fair I haven't a clue, what I do know is that most of the passengers had put their 'heads together' and did not turn up to get on the bus at the time arranged but an hour later, swearing that that was the time that they understood the bus was going. We clearly had a good time, for like good Welshmen who travel on buses we sang all the way home, to find that the owner of the yard had locked up and there was a 12 foot door between us and our bikes. Climbing onto my mate's shoulders I managed to scramble over, unlock the doors and wheel our bikes out. So as not to offend the owner we closed and locked the doors from inside, a low stone wall and the crossbars on the door providing a simpler way of getting out again—but the owner was puzzled and worried by 'disappearing bikes' until we are able to explain what happened.

Another time I was not so lucky. There was what we thought would be a good picture on 'in town' and my mate and I decided to go, but my fairy godmother, or more correctly my earthly Father, decided that this same field had to be cut around. This involved cutting one swathe around the edge of the field with the scythe and tying the corn so cut into sheaves so that the tractor and binder could then be taken in without the need to trample any corn down. I was terribly annoyed, annoyance that grew when it became wet and the cutting did not take place.

At this time we had no tractor of our own but a very good neighbour did a little contract corn cutting to the advantage of both of us. On one occasion when this took place, in a year in which we were overrun with rabbits, our ex-prisoner of war Ken was there with the twelve bore shotgun. As the corn was cut the rabbits' refuge disappeared and I'm afraid they had to pay their corn bill. To me that binder was the most wonderful machine in the world. It cut the corn by sweeping it onto a moving canvas that took it up and over the driving wheel where it was packed and tied into sheaves. Never again would I have to tie sheaves with straw bands, and never again would I have thistle pricks in my hands.

However, the corn cutting proved the last straw for the poor old horses. From that day on their time was in doubt, not just as far as we younger ones were concerned but the older generations as well. A point of no return arrived when a splinter of oak pierced one of the older horses' hind feet and poisoned the wound, forcing her to be retired. We needed either a new horse—or a tractor. The vote was two to one for a tractor. But with the tractor came need for new tackle, and as things improved so we acquired our set. A two furrow trailer plough was bought and a few 'Heath Robinson' modifications made to other equipment until such times as cash became available to purchase the proper machines.

Soon it was discovered that 'Down Country' farmers were selling second hand machinery and implements quite cheaply as they bought better and more up to the minute equipment.

In due course the motorcycle that had been ridden past the Scrap By Date and the car of a similar rating were replaced by a respectable car.

CHAPTER VI
Abbey-cwm-hir

There were two villages that featured in this time of my life—Llandewi, where I went to school, and Abbey-cwm-hir. The name of the latter village translates as the Abbey of the Narrow Valley. The abbey is that built in 1143 a little lower down the valley by Cistercian monks who sought isolated places with a good water supply. Incidentally the abbey once had the longest nave in Britain, reputed to have been 242 feet long.

After the Dissolution stone from the building was cannibalised to build and repair local churches including Llananno, where the old rood screen is preserved, and Llanbister and Llanidloes, as well as local farmhouses. Devannor was certainly built from abbey stone, as evidenced by a carved stone lintel over a doorway leading to the hall, and where an oak staircase with large newel posts is often mentioned as a relic from the abbey. Preserved in St. Harmon's church is a staff that is supposed to have been the property of the abbot.

The Cistercians were as near self supporting as the district would allow and it is possible that they introduced deer into the locality as one hill to the east of the village is still known as The Deer Park. Certainly they had their own fish breeding industry. Quite close to the abbey ruins there still exists a small lake that appears to be man-made, marked on Ordnance Survey maps as The Fish Pool, which probably held trout. About a mile to the north on the road to Bwlch-y-Sarnau is the Fishpools, one of the farms owned by the monks, and during their stay an earth wall was built to make a dam for a lake that covered several acres. Here the fish were farmed and from where mature fish were taken to be held

111

Devannor, almost certainly built with stone from the abbey at Abbey-cwm-hir

in the small lake close to the abbey until required. Over the course of 20 to 22 June 1936 the area was ravaged by thunder storms of unusual ferocity, with displays of lightning so brilliant that there were periods of continuous light even after nightfall—sheep could even be seen on the neighbour's fields across the valley, and when the lightning was behind the hills they were set out in profile like a cardboard cut out. The associated continuous rain saturated the ground, and at Fishpools Farm the extra weight of water against the dam proved too much for its softened and weakened structure, and the dam gave way. The floodwater swept away some local bridges and drowned a few animals in its progress down the Clywedog valley. A bicycle shed and three bicycles even had to be retrieved from downstream.

Even though the abbey is in ruins, one feels that this was a special place and even now it has a sense of tranquillity, as the monks must have discovered. Llewellyn is supposed to be buried here but there does seem to be some doubt about this.

At the west end of the village, and forming one complete angle of the T-junction with the road to Bwlch y Sarnau—loosely translated as The Pass of the Paved Ways—is a barn. The route into

112

The Cwm-hir Valley

Abbey-cwm-hir is an old drovers' road as may be proven by the name of the westernmost part of the village—Piccadilly. It seems to have been the custom of the drovers to name some of their stopping places after areas of London to which they took their cattle. Nowdays the area known as Piccadilly comprises the School (now closed), School Cottage and a pair of semi-detached dwellings which bear the name Piccadilly as their address.

The first school was set up by a Mr. Francis Aspinal Philips, though its whereabouts is uncertain. It moved to The Laundry as we know it, in 1857 and remained there until 1868 when the son of the founder, George Henry Philips, had the present school built, followed by a house for the teacher in 1875. Pupils were charged for their schooling, the better off paying 3d. per week, the not so well off 2d. and the workmen's children 1d. If this caused difficulty to the parents these fees were often re-funded. Nevertheless, for a family of five—a medium sized family in those days—the cost was high, and in some families the children would attend on a rota basis, in others the brightest went to school and the not so stayed at home to help their parents. Many pupils left school at the age of 11 so as to be able to earn a little money to help the family's budget.

Mr. George Philips was a great benefactor of the school and it is recorded that he bore much of the running costs and gave prizes to

113

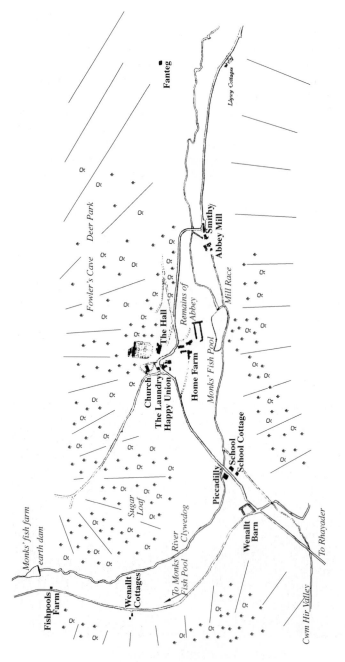

The layout of the village of Abbey-cum-hir

the pupils for excellence and good attendance. However, many of the reports of the performance of the children did not give a good overall impression of the school. Perhaps it was because the school was quite isolated, making it difficult to obtain qualified teachers— it is recorded that on more than one occasion the school was without a teacher for a time.

In 1917 Major Francis Philips, like his predecessors, took a lively interest in the school, most of the children being those of his own tenants. He provided the boys with two footballs, one to play with in school time and one to use in inter-school matches, which were generally with Bwlch-y-Sarnau on the Sports Day held on the level land adjacent to the ruins of the abbey. The squire also paid the childrens' expenses to enable them to attend the 'Intermediate' School in Llandrindod Wells.

This set-up was disturbed in 1922 when the Major accepted a grant for the school and then had a disagreement with the Education Authority. Being of an independent nature, and his family having built and largely financed the school till then, Major Philips closed the school after due notice and locked up the premises. After some elapse of time the children were taught in the vestry of Cefnpawl chapel, and a year after its closure the building was sold to Radnorshire County Council. (It was not the school we used, for others were nearer to where we lived.) Its subsequent history is like that for many schools in the county until, with family

School photo in 1923, at Cefnpawl

115

Molly Brown and her class at Abbey-cwm-hir in 1924

size decreasing and a declining school roll, the numbers of available pupils fell so low as to place the existence of the school in some doubt. In July 1969 the end came and the school finally closed.

Opposite the school was Piccadilly, a double dwelling. One part was occupied by Edward (Ted) Evans who was employed by Major Philips on the home farm as cowman, the other by Mr. J. Evans and family, Mr. Evans being referred to as Lacquer Jack. He had been a soldier in the Great War in which he had received a head wound which had needed a metal plate inserting, and hence his nick-name. He was employed by the Major as a chauffeur.

Further east, the Village Hall lies on the left. Built in the late 1930s, it is quite an imposing building for this purpose. It was clad in cedar shakes which have since been replaced by brick. At one end was a stage which could be broken down into tables for use in the hall, with front and wing curtains. Unfortunately there was no way across the hall behind the stage, and thereby hangs a tale.

The Penybont Young Farmers Club drama section staged a production of 'For Goodness Sake', a play about a family returning to Victorian times with a truly Autocratic Victorian father. This was put on at local parish and church halls to help boost their finances, the drama section only asking for expenses to be paid and a 'reward' of a cup of tea and a bun. Dresses for the most part had to be hired, but the dresses would not fit the waists or more correctly, the waists did not fit the dresses. Did those girls have to lose weight!

During the play one of the male characters had to exit from the right and then make a dramatic entry from the left. Luckily there were windows behind the 'wing' curtains, so once he had exited the stage he had to be got out through the right-hand window and back in through the left one. He managed alright and no-one would have been any the wiser, except that our leading man had an interview with the B.B.C. and the local electrician had wired us up so that the people in the hall could hear the broadcast between the acts. The conversation largely focussed on the difficulties that we had to overcome in producing our play in ill-equipped village halls!

Our real problem in this performance fell in another scene. The father, with a very prominent hirsute embellishment, had to roar onto the stage to deliver an appropriate condemnation of the actions of one of his daughters. In so doing, he drew a wisp of crepe hair into his mouth and proceeded to choke. Luckily the producer's wife took his place while he went off stage to try and disgorge half of his moustache. When we had just about come to the end of our ability to ad-lib, he returned looking like a boiled beetroot, his magnificent moustache lopsided, illkempt and bedraggled.

At the request of the local Mother's Union we were to also perform this play in the church hall in Llanbister, newly re-opened after being used as a store during the war, and conditions, through no fault of theirs, were to say the least primitive.

'For Goodness Sake' being performed at Abbey-cwm-hir,
with the author on the right

Penybont YFC Drama Group, with the author in the back row on the right, and his sister at the other end of the row

We arrived a couple of hours prior to opening time, with scenery and props and proceeded with the business in hand. After a while the vicar arrived, a six footer and no mistake, introduces himself and gives us the usual vicarish chat before telling us not to let anyone through the side door. 'It often happens that people try to get in for nothing by claiming that they are connected with the show. If any one tries it just say that you cannot let them in here and to go to the main entrance in the front of the hall'.

We get on with sorting out the props and our attire when there comes a knock at the door. As I was the only one anything like respectable, holding my trousers up with one hand I climbed up on the closed piano and opened the window to see a little chappie with a big black hat standing in the rain and darkness. He was very polite. 'Can I come in, please?'

I latched on and 'come over all polite like'. 'No, sir, I'm very sorry, sir'.

'But,' he says, 'I'm connected with the show'.

'Oh yes', I say, 'so am I'.

'But', he says, 'I am the vicar's brother'.

'And I am Charlie's aunt'.

'And I'm the vicar at Llanbadarn Fynydd'.

Me, not so polite now, 'And I'm the preacher from Maesyrhelem, so front door for you mister'.

With that our rather persistent gatecrasher took his leave.

At last all was ready and the Vicar of Llanbister came onto the platform to announce the play. Alongside him stood his little brother, the five-foot Vicar of Llanbadarn Fynydd. I could have crawled into a hole in the skirting. But all's well that ends well and after the play we had the usual cup of tea and a bun, and Vicar A and Vicar B were both very sociable and friendly.

Returning to the 'tour' of Abbey-cwm-hir, heading toward the village centre from the Village Hall there were some rather antiquated farm buildings on the right before the village proper is reached, with the Laundry and the Happy Union.

The Happy Union in 2001.
Note the 'Estate' windows

As mentioned, the laundry used to be the village school and school house combined. When it was closed as a school, the Hall employed people to 'do' their laundry in the building, and hence its name. The house that had been the residence of the school teacher now became that of the laundry man and laundress.

The pub The Happy Union stood on the opposite side of the road.

To enter it you have to turn off the road down a track into a walled yard which gave access to pub and the landlord's house on the right with the Post Office and shop immediately on your left. Up the stairs from the shop was a large room which served as a local function room before the Village Hall was built by Miss Christine Philips. It was in this room that the Boy's Club met. The membership fee was 2s. per annum which entitled you to play darts, rings (quoits), dominoes, cards, draughts (chequers) and snooker, in return for which the room was provided along with the games,

The sign of the Happy Union

the latter also owned by the Philips family it would appear. Lighting came from their generator, as did that for the whole village.

The Happy Union had an unusual sign to go with its unusual name. It depicted a man standing astride a goat with a platter of meat and a pint glass of ale, the goat symbolising hair and skin for clothing, meat for food and the ale for the thirst. Beer drawn from barrels set up on a trestle in sight of the customer was drawn off into a large jug, if the place was full, or into your glass, if not too busy. It was a place of reminiscence, thought, and story.

A South Wales timber firm would operate in the area when there was timber to be felled and hauled to the station, and they would often employ migrant labour who would take their relaxation in the pub. One fellow took a shine to a local spinster who had a reputation for being difficult to become acquainted with.

For a while it looked as if he would succeed where others had failed, but this was not to be. The suitor ran short of money in the pub one night and put her up for auction. The story reached her ears and an extended shelf life was indicated that went on to the final Sell By date.

It is often said that the Welsh way of speaking is backwards, and no doubt the Welsh think the same of the English way of putting things, but there was one Welshman who had lost a couple of young sheep, hogs to the initiated, and was making enquiries in the pub about them in hope of recovering them. On being asked what were they like he said, 'Well, one is a little 'un, an' t'other, well, a bit littler'.

The same farmer once had 51 hogs (in this instance, the previous year's lambs) to sell. The deal was reaching its final stage of so much per head, when the buyer, hoping to get the most for his money, says, 'If I give thee that, thee't have to give me one for luck'. The farmer walked in amongst the animals and sorted out a very small one. 'Alright, but let me tell thee that that is the one I be givin' thee for luck',—'luck' being a small rebate or gift by the seller to encourage a deal or bargain.

Across from the shop was the church built in the late 19th century by the local squire and equipped with an unusually good

Abbey-cwm-hir church from a postcard of the 1930s

pipe organ, which at this time was in good order. A private path connected the church to the grounds of the Hall.

This was occupied for many years by the Fowler family who had a reputation of being one of the wealthiest around. As an old rhyme has it:

> Poor Radnorshire, Poor Radnorshire
> Never a park and never a deer
> Never a Squire with five hundred a year
> Save Richard Fowler of Abbey-cwm-hir.

Their name is also remembered in Fowlers' Cave, more of an overhang than an actual cave, so I have been given to understand, the land now being occupied by the Forestry Commission and not easily accessible.

The Fowlers sold the estate to a Mr. Wilson who seems never to have taken up occupation. His investments in London turned sour and he soon had to sell again, the Philips family purchasing the estate in 1834. Sometime during the period when Major Philips was in residence at the Hall an incident occurred that was Hushed Up. There were two girls living with their parents in the village, one of whom had been going out with a farm lad from up the valley. From this farm there was an old cart track to the village which led over the back of the Sugar Loaf, a steep-sided hill, which was the route used by the lad on his courting forays. After they had been courting for some time the boy called for the girl one Saturday night, only to be told that she was ill with the 'flu. He called again the following Wednesday, to be told that she was a little better but was still in bed. He appeared again the next Saturday when it was raining cats and dogs, to find the mistress of the house and the other girl had gone visiting one of the neighbours, leaving the master sat by the fire with the girl who was supposed to be ill. He was told that she was still too ill to go out on such a night, and should stay in the warm. If he could return on Wednesday she should be fit to see him then.

Sunday morning dawned clear, bright and dry and the Major decided to go for a ride up on the hills so he gave orders to saddle his pony, a big fine hunter, and off he went up the track at the back of the church, the quickest way up to the high ground. Before he had gone very far he came across a newly dug hole on the back of the Sugar Loaf that looked suspiciously like the shape and size of a grave. Surprised and no doubt worried he hurried back to the village, and asked around to find if anyone knew anything about it, to see if it was something serious or some prankster playing a very sordid or macabre joke. No-one had any answers that made sense, so he ordered his men up there first thing on Monday morning to fill it in. By some means it was then discovered that the farm lad had dug the grave as he was sure that the girl had found another boy and was using the 'flu story to avoid him. What his true intentions were we can only guess.

At this time the owner of the Hall held significant sway over local affairs, and the Major told the lad that if he left the area immediately and promised by everything he held dear never to return, and never to attempt to see the girl again, the matter would be closed—even though no crime had actually been committed. The lad left to find work in Hereford.

People who have lived in the area a long time can still just about discern where the grave was dug, though it is ever less discernible from adjoining forestry work.

In general, however, the Major was the opposite of the popular conception of the landlord, and provided two local amenities. When the telephone came to Llandrindod Wells he decided to extend the lines to his house, with a further extension to the Post Office in Abbey-cwm-hir, feeling that the village needed a phone. This was a single wire system, the wire carried by a 'tent' insulator placed on the top of each pole. He also converted the mill, utilising the waterwheel to drive a dynamo that in turn charged a bank of batteries which supplied people in the village with electricity for a nominal fee. (On the approach to the village on a dark and windy night from a southerly direction you might encounter a strange phenomenon—a brilliant flash of lightning somewhere in the area of the ruins of the old abbey, followed by complete darkness enhanced by the brilliance of the preceding flash. But there was no thunder, just complete silence and if you weren't aware of the cause, your hair would start to stand on end, imagining some ghostly goings on amongst the ruins. What actually happened was that the lines carrying the electric current sagged over the years, and if the wind was of the right strength and direction, the wires were blown close enough for a short to occur in the vicinity of the abbey ruins. Should you be riding your bike at night and without lights towards the village when such a flash occurred, you just had to keep going at the speed you had already reached with not a clue as to where you were heading until your sight returned to normal!) This service continued until the village was connected to the national Grid in 1959. Believe it or not there were some who were not happy about these changes, though later they became quite proud of them.

To virtually everyone the Major was known as 'Sir', except by the Major's gardener. This man, known by the nick-name of Farmer, was of small of stature and was bandy-legged with it, which made him look smaller still. He had one love second to that of the garden, and that was his pipe, whether it was fired up or not. He was often teased that his pipe was not going very well, with the result that he used to draw on it to prove that it was. This continued until the tobacco was nearly in flames and with Farmer coughing his head off. Strangely enough he always fell for it, so perhaps he enjoyed doing it.

The Philips family also paid in full for the road to the village for the distance that it passed through the Estate and contributed a further half to where it joined the Newtown to Llandrindod Wells road. This was prior to the days when tarmac was thought of in this area, and when stone from the quarries on the farms adjacent to the road was used. In one place the bank of rock had to be cut away to make room for the road, leaving a rockface rising about a hundred feet on one side, and a sharp drop down to the river on the other. At the foot of this the river runs deep and the story goes that a lorry load of sugar once plunged down this drop and came to rest in the river. Needless to say that stretch of water is now known as the Sugar Pool. Whether the trout were any sweeter after than before nobody is saying; all I can say is that the trout out of the Sugar Pool taste just the same as any other.

During the 1914-18 war the Timber Supply Department removed a lot of timber from the hillsides and left the road in a shocking state, with huge wheel ruts left by the timber carriages that were a foot or so wider than the normal trap or carriage. Stone for the road's repair was hauled from the quarries and left in heaps on the roadside where it could be broken into smaller pieces with which to fill the ruts. One of these heaps was left near the entrance to the Hall. One of the wandering ex-soldiers, cast adrift by the war, offered to break up this particular pile and level the surrounding ruts. Major Philips, himself a veteran of the war, not only took him at his word but brought him bread, meat and ale to quench his hunger and his thirst—and left him with two stone breaking hammers. He offered the man 10 shillings to be paid as soon as he had finished the job, a magnificent sum for that amount of work.

When the Major thought that sufficient time had passed for the job to be nearing completion, he returned to the entrance and was surprised to see that there was no movement and no sound of hammer on stone. On further investigation he discovered that very little work had been done and that the man was missing along with the two hammers.

This was a rare occurrence as most of these wandering survivors of the war were honourable men who had suffered traumatic events and could not settle down. 'Of no fixed abode', they had an orbit of more or less a yearly span. One of them was the Riddle Mender, or at least that was what we called him due to the fact that we hadn't any other name for him, and of course that begs the question. When corn was threshed with a flail the result was a mixture of grain and chaff, and to separate this a 'winnower' was used that was made up of riddles or sieves of different sizes according to requirements. Even one larger hole instead of two or three little holes, due to rusting or some other failure, would allow rubbish to pass through and spoil the whole lot. When this happened there was no choice but to have the riddle re-wired at the cost of a penny per hole.

Air was blown across these riddles as they were shaken and as the seed dropped through them the hulls or chaff were blown away. The process was generally repeated, the first time (with a number one riddle) faster and with larger holes in the riddle, and the second time with smaller holes and slower. This resulted in clean seed ready for storage. A number one riddle had holes one and a half inches square, so cost 5s. 4d. per square foot to repair. However, the smallest riddle, that for wheat had holes one eighth of an inch square. That cost the same to repair a square inch as a number one for a square foot!

Another rare visitor was the Clogger, a buyer of alder trees from which to make clogs for factory workers. Alder was highly suitable as the wood was light in weight yet had good insulating properties. These trees grew in profusion alongside the river and were cut when the sap was down and then taken away to dry.

One of this fraternity of periodical travellers was a complete mystery. He was well dressed with a collar and tie, his shoes were always brightly polished, and he was well spoken. All he ever wanted

One of the characters of the area—Archie, with his dog Turk.
Archie had apparently once played football for Arsenal, but became a
drover, sleeping with Turk wherever the day's work ended. Of the two, Turk
was the smarter: coat shining, ears and tail up and happy as the day was
long, as many of their days were. However, one had to die before the other,
and this lot fell to Archie. Turk never got over it, and it was eventually,
and reluctantly, decided that it would be an act of mercy
for Turk to follow his missing master

was to sleep the night in the hay, whereupon, without being asked,
he would hand over his pipe and box of matches as security against
him staring an accidental fire. At 7a.m. we would find him having a

wash in the cattle trough, before he brushed his clothes and polished his shoes. I will always remember him giving his shoe a few brushes and then spinning the brush to change ends and give a few more strokes before again spinning the brush to reverse ends. I shall never cease to wonder what he was or where he was going but I am certain that he was a gentleman of the first order.

However, there was one person we did not care to see, who was more of a peddler than a tramp and always had a case of tie pins, brooches, cheap rings and watch chains. The problem was that when you bought something from him he began to think that you were a 'soft touch' and would start to pressurise you, becoming a little belligerent. Once I was unlucky enough to meet him on the road that ran through the farm when I was on my own. You never had money in your pockets on the farm, and he became really difficult because I couldn't, or as he thought wouldn't, buy. If it hadn't been for Shep, the sheepdog, whom I had to keep in check, I felt as if I might have suffered an injury. Fortunately I never saw him again.

But he was the exception to the rule. Often all they wanted was somewhere warm to sleep, a can full of tea and a bit of bread and cheese, little enough for people who had risked their lives and lost their stability for the likes of us who were lucky not to have suffered.

Quite a common sight in those days was to see one of their number sitting at the side of the road with a small fire over which was suspended a fair sized tin with a wire handle hanging from a bended stick, in which they were boiling a drop of water to make themselves a cup of tea. There would always be a small piece of stick or a matchstick floating on the water in the tin as this was supposed to avoid the tea getting 'smoked'—something that did occasionally occur even when boiling water over an open fire in the home.

There were also the local old soldiers who had their own particular character. It is said that Major Francis Philips and only a very few of his company were able to return to the British lines after being completely surrounded, but as far as I am aware he never spoke of his experiences. He never married and was a loner in some respects, yet he built up his estate and maintained a full complement of staff to run it.

The blacksmith was another survivor of the Great War, and had the distinction of driving a captured German tank back to the British lines. He was much cleverer than most people realised, with a seeming ability to do any job or sort out any problem machine that came his way.

One local farmer, known to be particularly penny-pinching when it came to paying his bills, had installed an oil engine to cut chaff and thresh his corn. This engine had to be started and 'fed' with petrol for a short time before turning to paraffin oil, so as to generate sufficient heat to vaporise the oil. As paraffin was much cheaper than petrol, this farmer would attempt to make the engine run on oil before it was hot enough, resulting in an oiled-up sparking plug. So the blacksmith was called in to remedy the unknown fault. Having sized up the position, he asked for a nice clean rag, knowing that the farmer would probably have to go and beg such a thing off his wife. Whilst the farmer was away on his errand, the blacksmith took out the sparking plug and cleaned it up. Back came the farmer with his rag, and the blacksmith went through a routine of wiping around the top of the plug and the end of the high tension lead, then said, 'Give it a try now', and it duly started.

'Thanks a lot', says the farmer, 'do you want that bit of rag?'

'Sure', he is told. 'I'll keep that for next time', knowing that that is all the pay he is likely to get, and that on the next occasion the farmer would have to find another piece of cloth and spend quite a bit of time wiping around the plug and the lead to no purpose.

The next time he was called out to have a look the blacksmith took an old sparking plug with him, all polished up and shining. After due deliberation and investigation he announced that a new plug was the only cure this time—at a cost of 10 shillings, then the equivalent of several gallons of petrol—and which he proceeded to fit, this time in full view of the farmer, Finally he advised the farmer to use a lot more petrol when starting to avoid spoiling this special new plug.

Another local was Old Bill—quarryman, road maker and general repair man. He was happiest when repairing farm roads and farmyards. It is told of him that one day he approached Major Philips and brought to his notice the poor condition of the farm-yard at Cefnpawl farm and suggested that he should see about getting stone to put matters right. He received a sympathetic hearing and the Major asked how much would it take.

'There wants thousands of tons there sir', to which the Major was silent. Bill repeated 'Hundreds of tons sir', but still the silence remained. In desperation Bill said, 'Nine or ten sir, for sure!', and as the saying goes, got the job.

Bill had a little deformity, in that one ear was smaller than the other and had been that way from birth. Arriving for work one New Year, maybe after a heavy night for something had disturbed his usual good humour, he was greeted with a wish of 'A Happy New Year', to which he is supposed to have responded with 'And a Happy New Nose to you too'.

During the Second World War a few 'strange' people ended up in the country districts, often ones who were not fit for National Service but were anxious to do their bit in any way they could. Often because of their lack of experience they were thought as oddities, as in fact some were.

One couple, no doubt of good family as they had sufficient cash to buy a farm, did so and proceeded to learn the hard way. The farmhouse had a lovely situation, with a beautiful view down the valley, but it was a long way from a surfaced road. They lacked the experience to select good stock, with the result that their stock were not good sellers, and their team of horses were not equal to their tasks on a steep hill farm. Yet they did what they set out to do even if in a slightly unorthodox way—for example they milked their house cow out in the field, or wherever she happened to be at the relevant time—and made a living without being a nuisance or a worry to their neighbours, which is more than can be said for some farmers. During the Whinberry (or Wimberry in the local dialect) season this couple could be seen in the early morning each mounted on one of their team with a bucket in front of them. This contained their sandwhiches for their day long session on the hill picking whinberries, and in the afternoon the sandwiches had been replaced by a fill of berries—which was no mean achievement as anyone who has tried this can tell you.

In the Twenties and Thirties anyone looking through the trees towards Abbey-cwqm-hir's Hall from the road by the church would have noticed a large box-like structure high in the trees. This was a meat safe, for there were no fridges in those days, at least not in rural areas, which was raised and lowered by a system of pulleys and remained cool in the leafy shade.

One day the local repair man had to remove the oil tank from the Hall to repair a leak, and had it taken to the 'square' in front of the church where he proceeded to solder up the offending hole. All

Abbey Farm, from a postcard of the 1920s

went well for a short time, and then the tank exploded. Fortunately the man escaped unhurt, and the tale goes that the tank's brass tap was found behind the church—but the tank was never found.

Standing on this square one is as near as can be in the centre of the village. Looking east the Hall occupies the dominant position, built as it is on higher ground, and being an imposing structure does tend to dwarf the other houses in sight.

From here the road bends right bounded by stone walls, a high one on the Hall side and a low one on the other behind which were in general rather pretty gardens. This is The Paddock, the theory being that previous to the houses being built this was the piece of land where the Fowlers kept their carriage horses.

A little way on and straight in front is the Home Farm, farmed by the squire with the help of a waggoner, cowman and several handimen who doubled up as estate workers. It was here that my grandfather learned his trade as a carpenter / joiner when he was young.

The windows of the greater part, if not the whole of the estate had distinctive iron-frames forming small panes, with the ironwork near the top bending over to form arches that linked with each other (see the photo of the Happy Union on p.119). It may be that they were fitted by the first Philips, Francis Philips, who was an iron factor from Manchester and who was responsible for a lot of the improvements and re-building of the houses on the estate, using iron products from his own factory.

From near the entrance drive to the Hall the road is at its highest point in the village from where it takes quite a long southwards gradient down to a sharp right over a bridge and then a sharp left to follow the other side of the river. Quite a number of motorists have made a surprise visit to the wheelwright's garden even if that was not their intention. For situated by the bend are the carpenter/wheelwright's, the blacksmith's and the mill, part of the estate and sharing the collective name of Frog Town. Where or how this name originates I still have to find a believable reason.

Travelling south again was the Tunnel, a couple of hundred yards of road where the trees on each side had grown over until completely covering the road to such an extent that even on a brilliant summer day it was cool and dark in there. Sadly, a severe gale blew a lot of them down and the effect was lost.

Further on are two cottages that were originally houses for estate workmen, but as less people were required, one of the cottages had been let to a man who made his living gathering and selling moss to florists for wreaths and flower displays. Both the occupants were keen gardeners. The cottages were built on a gentle slope facing the road in a way that was ideally situated for floral display, and display they did in no uncertain fashion.

The moss gatherer had a Standard car with a trailer behind and we always gave him and his car a wide berth—for he had only one eye and his judgment of distance was none too clever. Several times I had the doubtful honour of getting his car started as he was often confused as to which knob did what—let alone the pedals. To me he was a useful man to have in the district, for he had an extensive collection of easy-reading books, which you could borrow for nothing, in fact he seemed pleased to have you borrow them, which was very acceptable when it was six miles to the library in Llandrindod Wells. It was rumoured that he had two wives, but this was never substantiated.

Down on the left by the river is a cottage, the Fanteg, unseen and unknown for the most part. A Miss Davies lived there, herself seldom seen and a bit of a mystery as far as we were concerned.

A distance from the road up the bank on the right lies Cefnpawl, at one time a very large sheep run. Up to the early 19th century a lot of the hill land was unenclosed when, according to some reports, some of this open land was appropriated by people in the legal profession who had the know-how in these matters; a case where the pen was wielded with more power than the sword. All the farm-houses in the district had stone floors and the 'Flag' stones were quarried on Rhiw Gam then part of Cefnpawl farm. The cost was supposed to be 1s. 6d. each.

One gruesome crime was, however, committed at Cefnpawl. As with many farms in the locality, on this particular holding a waggoner and cowman were employed. The cowman had the repu-tation for being a penny or two short of a pound, whilst the waggoner certainly was not and, as is often the case, took advantage of it. No doubt it started with a little harmless teasing, but finding that satisfying, he began to increase the 'play' until the stage was reached when the cowman became extremely annoyed. How long this took no-one knows, as the waggoner was careful not to do anything when there were other people about. One night the cowman finally reached breaking point. He stayed downstairs until all but he had gone to bed, then took the farmer's shotgun, loaded it, went upstairs and shot the waggoner in bed, before fleeing to a nearby farm where he was subsequently arrested and where the shotgun was found. Charged with the murder, the defence success-fully argued that the cowman was insane, and he avoided the hangman's rope, instead being detained during 'His Majesty's Pleasure'.

A little further down is the entrance to the Brickyard, now two dwellings but an indication of the comprehensive nature of the local economy in previous years.

Travelling on there is a sign for Devannor, which was used as a meeting place for the Methodists for many years as a result of their persecution by the established churches. The non-conformists usually held their meetings in isolated farmhouses, often changing their venue in an effort to remain undetected. Not far along is the Baptist Chapel, and here again the hand of the Hall was apparent. As there was no Baptist Chapel in the district, the Philips family gave a piece of land and built a chapel of cut stone with sandstone corners, cornices and window surrounds. The inside was made from beautifully carved and polished wood. The building was provided with underfloor heating, the aisles having a walkway of figured grating allowing the heat to percolate up through into the chapel. Each pew had a handle and tray for wet umbrellas or walking sticks.

To me its crowning glory was a rose widow of stained glass coupled with side windows containing lead-glazed diamond-shaped coloured glass. All this was provided by a family who were High Church. Sadly the chapel no longer exists, having become dangerous and been demolished.

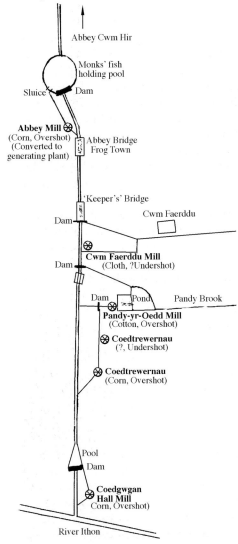

Plan of the mills near Abey-cwm-hir

Further on again are the Cuckoo Gate and the Cuckoo Oak, where the cuckoo is first reputed to sing in the county of Radnorshire each year. The oak is only just surviving. It was near here, during the occupation of the Fowlers, that a man built a house without the family's consent. To regularise matters Mr. Fowler bought the place off him for £18, then charged him rent!

A hundred yards further on is the Keeper's Lodge, at the eastern end of the estate.

In the late Twenties, the road from this eastern boundary was just broken stone padded and packed by the passage of many hooves—the squire and the vicar were the only car owners. Cwm faerddu is on the left shortly after Keeper's Lodge and a small stream flowed by the farmhouse and passed under the road, which it travelled a short distance alongside, boosted by

The now dry mill stream which once carried water through our farm to Pandy-yr-Oedd Mill

another stream, then turned at right angles to head straight for the river Clwedog. Before it reached the river its power was once used by a mill, a fulling mill the records state, but little or no evidence of this mill remains today.

For a while road and river run more or less parallel and soon reaches Henfryn, the seat of this narrative, where the Pandy joined

Coedtrewernau Mill in 2001

End of the overshot mill at Coedtrewernau showing the hole in the wall for the drive from the wheel to the mill inside

the Clwedog. Near this juncture, where the road runs along a raised embankment, originally a dam built to contain water, was another mill—Pandy-yr-Oedd, the Mill of the Cotton.

As far as I can discover there were five and possibly six mills in the vicinity, two of them within a hundred yards of each other, the first an undershot and the second an overshot. The gear-wheels of the latter are formed of wood, presumably of oak, with iron-banding at the points of extreme stress, as was all mill gearing until iron and steel came into general use around 1850. The grinding stones are still in evidence, but the iron waterwheel was commandeered during the last war. If there were two mills here and one at Pandy it meant that there were three mills within half a mile, and six water driven mills in a distance of five miles (not to mention the corn mill at Llandewi), comprising three corn and two cotton or cloth mills, together with one of unknown purpose, all on or on feeders of the Clwedog.

The story goes that a Mr. Meredith, a cotton factor from Manchester considered that there was a market for his goods in the area and to further this purpose purchased three adjoining farms to secure a permanent supply of water to drive his mills. The Pandy supplied water in the first instance, and there is some indication that this supply was augmented by water brought from a little higher up the river Clwedog and brought to the mill by a Mill Flem—the local name for a man-made stream for this purpose.

Our farm contained traces of a channel (now looking a little uncertain) that had its origin half a mile or so upstream of the Clwedog and led to Pandy's Mill Pool. It is fair to assume that this was to supplement the water supplied by Pandy, which tended to become very low in a long hot dry spell. After the water had worked this mill, it was returned to Pandy to travel a few yards before being dammed and diverted southwards by another Flem in the direction of Coedtrewernau where there were two mills. The first was an undershot mill, a working corn mill in the early twentieth century, the last miller being a man by the name of Sam Brown. From here the water was taken on a raised channel to an overshot wheel, and thence back to the Clwedog. The water was again used after it had joined the Clwedog at Coedgwgan Hall mill. This mill, like the corn mill at Abbey-cwm-hir, has been in use within living memory.

The cloth mills are understandable with the local concentration of sheep farming. Indeed, 'Pandy' means a fulling mill, which was used for the production and thickening of cloth. Less than a mile upstream there was another cloth mill, possibly producing cloth for wear.